Trauma Theory & Testimony

Breaking Cycles Through Lived Experience and Developmental Theory

A Textbook Memoir

By

Charlietta D. Owens, MSW, LGSW, CTP

ISBN (Paperback): 979-8-9938495-8-4

Library of Congress Control Number: 2025924058

Published by The Owens Publishing House LLC

Faribault, MN

Table Of Content

Disclaimer

This book is a combination of memoir and educational content. It is intended for informational and educational purposes only and should not be considered professional mental health, medical, or legal advice. The author and publisher make no representations or warranties with respect to the accuracy or completeness of the contents and specifically disclaim any implied warranties of fitness for a particular purpose. Readers should consult qualified professionals for guidance specific to their own circumstances. The author and publisher shall not be held liable for any damage arising directly or indirectly from the use of the material contained herein. The author and publisher have changed the names of some of the individuals in this book to protect their privacy. The individuals whose names are used have agreed to have their names mentioned in this book.

Dedication

To Gwen and Charles Kirklen, my parents—thank you for giving me life, even when life itself felt heavy. I honor the difficulty of our story, the pain, and the beauty intertwined. Your struggles shaped my strength, and your absence, during the time I lived without you, taught me presence. I carry both the wounds that may have scarred my heart and the wisdom I gained from every moment you took time to teach me. I hold these not in resentment but in truth. This book is not written to cause harm or bring shame—but to bring insight, authenticity, and healing. It is important for you to know that I remember, I forgive, and I love with my whole heart.

To Shawn Owens, my husband—you met me not at my polished, presentable best but in the heart of my trauma. You loved the parts of me the world said were too hard, too complex, and too broken. It was the only kind of love that I could deal with at that time in my life. And that love? It didn't just comfort me—it helped me rise. You held my most painful secrets close to you. Everything I've built—this legacy, this healing, this book—is laced through with your quiet strength. The safety of your presence gave me courage to tell my story without fear, to step into my purpose with both feet, and to become the woman I dared to imagine.

We overcame not just obstacles but odds. Each test we faced stood through time. And I'm grateful beyond words for a love that doesn't erase the past—but walks alongside it. Those memories are marked with weakness or strength. This legacy is not only mine, but it stands on your shoulders too—built upon support, guidance, and solidity.

To my children,

You are the reason I kept getting back up.

When the world counted me out, I counted you in.

When shame tried to write the ending, your faces reminded me the story wasn't over.

I clawed my way out of cycles, out of statistics, out of silence—because I refused to let trauma raise you, but somehow, it still showed up. I was determined to change the blueprint of what we know as generational curses.

You've watched me grind, cry, study, pray, and persevere. You've seen me in courtrooms and classrooms, in tears and in triumph. That wasn't just survival—it was strategy. Every degree, every promotion, every barrier I broke was for you. So you could walk through doors without wondering if they'd slam shut.

But more than that—I wanted you to know who I am, fully. Not just the professional titles or the put-together days. I want you to know about the grit it took to rebuild a life, about the faith that held me steady when I was scared, about the moments I almost gave up but didn't.

You are my proof that healing ripples. That legacy doesn't have to be pain passed down—it can be strength multiplied. If you ever feel unworthy, remember who your mama is. And remember who you are.

I didn't just survive for you. I soared so you could see what flying looks like.

How to Read This Book

To my readers—thank you for showing up. Whether you come to these pages as a student, a practitioner, or someone searching for your own reflection, this book is meant to meet you where you are.

This isn't a linear story, and I don't expect you to move through it in a straight line. Each chapter stands on its own with a theme, lived experience, and trauma-informed theory woven together. Read it front to back or jump to the parts that speak to you in the moment.

Use the charts, diagrams, and references at the end of each chapter to deepen your understanding. Let the stories slow you down. Let the theory sharpen your lens. And let both challenge what you thought you knew about trauma, resilience, and healing.

If you leave these pages believing that transformation is possible—that trauma doesn't get the final say—then this book has done its work.

This isn't the end of my story. But it can be the beginning of understanding what healing could look like, if it resonates with you.

Acknowledgments

To Gwen and Charlie, my parents—thank you for giving my children the childhood I never had. I honor the healing that time has brought, and the love you pour into the next generation. My heart is so full. Watching you nurture them has softened parts of me I didn't even know were still aching.

Mommy, you are my rock. You showed me how to be a provider for my home. You showed me how to love hard. You have showed up for me in ways I didn't think anyone could. You showed me your heart and how to give with no condition. Not only have you slid folded-up bills (whether they were $5, $10, $20, $100) in my pocket when no one was looking; you have also slid little gems down for me that I didn't realize I had picked up. I admire you deeply.

Daddy, you have always given me hard talks, but nevertheless words of wisdom. I carry every word, conversation, and lecture with me. I need you to know that I remember the times you would pop-up out of nowhere when we were placed at Aunt's house and gave me long talks, telling me to protect my younger sister and brother. I remember you telling me you would be leaving to go to prison, and I would have to look out for them. I remember you saying to that little boy that was climbing on the clothing line poles with me in the back yard that time to get away from your daughter. I must have been about 11 years old.

My deepest gratitude to you both is that, because of the hard work you put in, my children will never know my trauma. Your care is a redemption story all on its own.

To Ingrid Haynes, my sister—thank you for holding my youngest baby at the time when prison held me. You carried their laughter, their tears, their routines, and their dreams. You gave them stability in the storm and gave me hope in the dark. I will never forget the weight you bore so I could rise again.

To Keyaira Williams, my sister—thank you for stepping in when my world was falling. You took my children before jail could take me, and in doing so, you gave them continuity, safety, and love. That act was more than sacrifice—it was sisterhood in its highest form.

To Vern Robinson, my aunt—who took in not just me but my siblings and my children as well—thank you for being the net that caught generations. You held us when systems failed us, fed us when cupboards were bare, and loved us when love felt threatened. Your home was our protection, and your heart was our inheritance. Thank you.

To Deb Eagle, my mentor—thank you for seeing the leader in me before I could claim her. You didn't just guide my career, but you also nurtured my voice, challenged my thinking, and reminded me that proximity is power. Your wisdom shaped not only my work but also my walk.

To Betty Davis, my aunt—thank you for showing me that change is possible. For standing up for me when my world was young. For being there for me when I needed you physically, financially, verbally, and emotionally. I admire your transformation; it's stuck with me.

To all 12 of my siblings and to my cousins—thank you for your unconditional love. Thank you for showing up at times when no one else would. Thank you for allowing me to show up as my authentic self every time. Thank you for creating the experiences we had. Our paths may not have the smoothest roadway, but we laid it one brick at a time. We all have a story of our own, but one thing we know is that our unique experiences hold so much pain, happiness, and love, "emphasis on 'love.' " From sharing bunk beds to big hearty meals together, from singing childhood songs to playing spades at the card tables, our memories will forever be cherished. I love each and every last one of you with my whole heart.

The photo displayed on the book cover is of the author and her father together. The photo displayed on the dedication page of this book is of the author and her mother together.

Purpose

Why This Book Exists?

This book was written to do more than just tell a story—it was written to teach.

I've lived through systems that were never designed for my healing. Foster care. Incarceration. Poverty. Racism. I've survived them, studied them, and now I work inside them. That full-circle journey is what gives this book its power.

Each chapter pairs personal narrative with developmental theory—Erikson's, Maslow, Freud, Piaget, and more—because I want readers to understand how trauma shapes development, and how resilience rewrites it. This isn't just a memoir. It's a curriculum. A resource. A tool for students, educators, and anyone trying to understand the human spirit beyond statistics and diagnoses.

I wrote this for psychology classrooms. For social work students. For system-involved parents. For case workers who want to do better. For survivors who need to feel seen. For anyone who's ever asked, "How did they end up like that?" and is ready to learn the answer.

This book is proof that lived experience is valid expertise. That theory comes alive when it's rooted in truth. And that healing isn't just possible—it's powerful.

At one point, I was the case. Now I carry them.

And this is the legacy I'm building—one chapter, one lesson, one life at a time

Teaching Note

Trauma Theory & Testimony is designed to serve both as personal testimony and as a structured teaching text. The book integrates developmental theory with lived experience so that students can see how abstract models connect to real-life trauma and resilience.

Each chapter includes:

- **Charts and Figures** — Visual summaries of developmental theories (Freud, Piaget, Erikson's, Maslow, Bowlby, Ainsworth) to anchor learning.
- **Themes** — A guiding statement at the start of each chapter to frame reflection.
- **Discussion Questions** — Prompts that encourage analysis, classroom dialogue, and application to casework.
- **Lessons in Practice** — Bridges between testimony and theory, highlighting practical implications.

Supporting materials include an APA-style reference list, glossary of terms, and curated resource list. Together, these elements allow the text to function as a curriculum tool for courses in psychology, social work, and human services, while also remaining accessible to general readers and community practitioners.

Introduction

Theme: This isn't just a memoir—it's a design.

I didn't write this book to relive my past. I wrote it to reframe it.

For years, I carried stories that felt too heavy to speak aloud. But as I studied Freud, Maslow, Erikson's, Piaget, Ainsworth, and Bowlby, I began to see my life not just as a series of traumas but as a record of development, resilience, and transformation. The theories weren't distant anymore—they were personal. They explained the silence, the survival, the scars. And they helped me understand how I kept growing, even when the world expected me to stay down.

This memoir is my contribution. It's part testimony, part teaching tool. Each chapter pairs lived experience with developmental theory, inviting readers to see how childhood neglect, incarceration, and systemic racism intersect with psychological growth. You'll find my story told in tight, honest scenes—followed by theory, reflection, and discussion questions. Because this isn't just about what happened. It's about what it means.

I write as a former client of the child welfare system, Master of Social Work (MSW), licensed graduate social worker (LGSW), and certified trauma professional (CTP)—as a mother, a former foster parent, a child welfare scholar, and a survivor. I write to honor the pain, but also to highlight the path forward. My goal is simple: to help students, educators, and system-involved families understand not just the "what" of human behavior—but the "why."

If you're reading this as a student, I hope it helps you see your future clients more clearly. If you're reading this as a survivor, I hope it reminds you that your story is worth telling. And if you're reading this as someone working inside the system, I hope it challenges you to listen deeper, act bolder, and never forget the humanity behind the file.

This book is not a confession. It's a curriculum. And every chapter is a lesson in what it means to break cycles, build legacy, and rise with purpose.

CHAPTER 1

He Told Me to Grab My Coat

Theme: Abandonment teaches its lessons early—long before a child can name the loss.

I always wanted to go with him. If he said no, I whined until he got tired of hearing me. But this time, I didn't even have to ask. On his way out the door, he told me, "Run back and grab your coat—we're going somewhere." I lit up. But when I came back, he was gone—and all that was left was my screaming and hollering. The kind that hurts your throat and swells your eyes shut. I fell for it again.

I didn't care that my coat was upside down by the time I raced back into the living room, ready to go, only to catch the front door slowly closing. I could hear the doorknob latch softly shut. I was only two, but I remember how soggy the couch became from my tears and saliva dripping down my face. Some would fall into my ears and onto the pillow where I lay, as I dramatically turned from one side to the other. I can still feel trickery in my brain. I pieced it together. He sent me back there on purpose so he could hurry up and leave.

Mama's smack on the backside of my thigh didn't make the screaming any better. "Shut up," she said. "He'll be back." But that didn't stop my crying. Mama would always dress me in these cute one-piece short outfits that tie on each of my shoulders. This gave her easy access to my legs.

The door didn't slam. That's how I knew it was intentional—he didn't rush or rage. He just stepped out quietly, like a whisper. Like he was sneaking away from something he never planned to face.

The living room glowed with that dusty afternoon light, where everything turns gold but feels no warmth. The TV buzzed in the background; nobody was watching it. The air smelled like old cigarettes from Mama and Daddy train-smoking all day. I turned side to side not to comfort myself but to survive the noise inside—the pounding heartbeat, the betrayal, the question: Why would he do that?

The couch was rough and textured beneath me. It always left indented marks engraved in my skin when I'd wake up from a good nap. This wasn't a good nap. I cried so long that the tears became a slow leak—less panic, more surrender.

I didn't have words yet for betrayal, but my body knew. My throat burned from screaming, and my baby brain worked overtime to solve what wasn't solvable—how do you make someone stay?

Mama's steady patting on my back eventually calmed me. I lay on my stomach, whining, with my voice matching the rhythm of her lenient hits. The pattern of it finally soothed me to sleep. Usually, it was my thumb that did the trick, but she'd snatch it out of my mouth anytime she caught me with it. This wasn't the first time Daddy tricked me. And it wasn't the last time Mama eased me. By the age of three, I already knew what being left out felt like.

That day taught me that hysterically crying wouldn't help me get what I wanted. It taught me not to believe anything anyone said and if it came true, I was surprised. I learned not to trust anyone around me. I learned how to put up walls.

Even as I grew older, I held on to this experience and didn't realize how this experience laid the very foundation for me to believe I wasn't enough for anyone.

As a little girl, I remember wondering all the time where my mom and dad were. Most of the time they were right there, but they were never present. They may have been in the house, but they would be in the room all day getting high or maybe they were mingling with friends or family. I always knew something was missing, but I couldn't quite put my finger on it.

Sometimes I wonder how much of those early memories are stitched from fragments—like patches sewn together by feeling rather than fact. I was only two, but the sound of that doorknob clicking shut has lived with me longer than most lullabies. By the time I was older, I realized the pattern had never really stopped—it had only changed form. It wasn't until then that I understood that my attachment style was fearful avoidant (Bretherton, 1992; Bowlby, 1982).

Mama and Daddy didn't always leave through the front door. Sometimes they left by locking themselves inside their bedroom, disappearing for hours while my siblings and I sat on the couch outside the room calling, "Mama . . . Mama . . . I'm hungry . . ." until our voices cracked. We'd whisper to each other, make up games in the house, anything to pass the time while that closed door answered us with silence.

It didn't matter if the sun rose and fell before they came out. We stayed there anyway, waiting like time might bend if we were patient enough. That silence was its own kind of abandonment. They were near, but they weren't present. The walls between us might as well have been miles apart.

I don't remember much about the projects, but I remember the playground in the backyard. The metal slides burned hot under the summer sun, the swings squeaked until you thought they'd snap, and the kids played like they belonged to one another. I remember running across that gravel, trying to keep up, even when my shoes slipped and skinned my knees. Out there, I didn't think about the girl left crying on the couch, or the one calling at a locked door that never opened. For a few moments, I was just an ordinary child, pushing off the ground and reaching for the sky, even if my arms were too short to hold it.

But inside the house, absence had a smell, a rhythm, a weight. It smelled like cigarettes and burnt spoons, sounded like muffled music behind a closed door, and pressed heavy in my chest like an anchor I couldn't shake off. I didn't have the words for addiction or neglect yet, but I knew the ache of waiting. I knew the sting of realizing that being in the same room as someone doesn't always mean you have them.

That lesson started when I was two with a coat and a quiet door, but it replayed over and over through my childhood. Sometimes I think that's why I clung to the smallest scraps of attention—because deep down, I already knew I wasn't enough to keep them close.

Theory in Practice: What Was Missing

Erikson's First Stage: Trust vs. Mistrust:

Children aged 0–18 months develop trust through consistency and warmth (Erikson, 1963). My father's unpredictable departures disrupted this stage. I didn't just experience absence—I experienced betrayal. Mistrust took root before I ever knew the word.

Piaget's Sensorimotor Stage:

At two years old, I was still learning object permanence—understanding that people exist even when not visible (Piaget, 1952; Huitt & Hummel, 2003). But trauma accelerated my cognition. I wasn't just noticing absence—I was interpreting intent. I felt tricked, because I was.

Maslow's Hierarchy of Needs:

Safety and stability sit at the base of Maslow's pyramid (Maslow, 1943). That day, I was emotionally unsafe. My body responded with shaking, crying, gasping. My need for reliable caregiving wasn't met, and that shaped how I sought connection for years to come.

Freud's Oral Stage:

Freud believed infants self-soothe through oral behaviors—nursing, sucking, crying (Freud, 1961). I wasn't just loud—I was regulating. My thumb, my voice, my motion were all survival tools. Later, I'd cope through sucking my thumb, quietly observing, and biting nails.

Lessons from a Toddler's Terror

Even before I could speak in full sentences, I understood abandonment. That feeling didn't live in my head—it lived in my throat, my chest, my belly. I didn't know how to name it yet, but I remembered how it taught me to be on guard, even at two.

Discussion Questions

1. How does early caregiver abandonment affect a child's ability to develop trust in others?
2. Can trauma accelerate a child's cognitive and emotional development?
3. Which developmental stages are reflected in this chapter, and how were they interrupted?
4. What are some ways children self-soothe when emotional support isn't available?
5. Recall a time when you learned something without being taught—how did the experience shape you?

Comparative Overview of Human Development and Attachment Theories

Figure 1.1

Sigmund Freud's Psychosexual Stages of Development

Stage	Age Range	Erogenous Zone	Developmental Descriptions
Oral	Birth – 1 year	Mouth	Sucking, biting
Anal	1 – 3 years	Anus	Toilet training
Phallic	3 – 6 years	Genital	Identity with same-sex parent
Latency	6 – 12 years	Dormant	Socialization
Genitals	12+ years	Genitals	Intimacy, reflection

Figure 1.2

Lawrence Kohlberg's Stages of Moral Development

Levels	Age Range	Stage
Pre-conventional	3 – 7 years	Obedience and Punishment
Conventional	8 – 13 years	Social Approval and Law & Order
Post-conventional	13+ years	Social Contract and Universal Ethics

Figure 1.3

Jean Piaget's Cognitive Development of Moral Development

Stage	Age Range	Developmental Descriptions
Sensorimotor	Birth–2 years	Senses and Motor Coordination
Preoperational	2–7 years	Symbolic Thinking
Concrete Operational	7–11 years	Logic with Concrete Objects
Formal Operational	11+ years	Abstract Reason

Figure 1.4

Erik Erikson Psychosocial Stages of Development

Stage	Age Range	Developmental Descriptions
Infancy	Birth–1 year	Trust vs. Mistrust
Early Childhood	1–3 years	Autonomy vs. Shame/Doubt
Preschool	3–6 years	Initiative vs. Guilt
School Age	6–12 years	Industry vs. Inferiority
Adolescent	12–18 years	Identity vs. Role Confusion
Young Adulthood	18–40 years	Intimacy vs. Isolation
Middle Adulthood	40–65 years	Generativity vs. Stagnation
Maturity	65+ years	Ego Integrity vs. Despair

Comparative Overview of Human Development and Attachment Theories

Figure 2.1
Abraham Maslow's Hierarchy of Needs

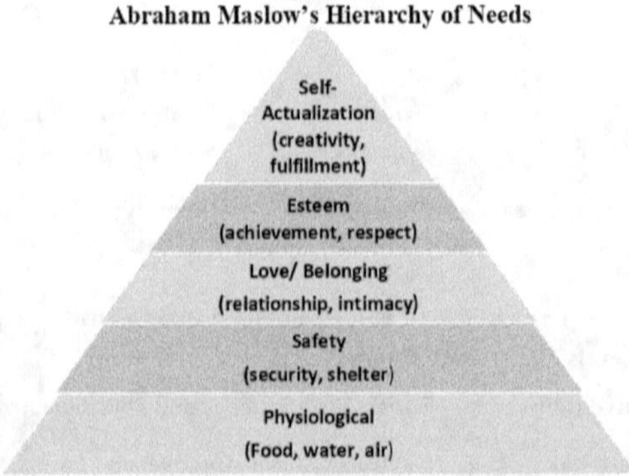

Figure 2.2
John Bowlby's Four Phases of Attachment

Phase	Age Range	Description
Pre-attachment	Birth-6 weeks	Infants show no specific attachment; respond to anyone.
Attachment-in-the-making	6 weeks - 6/8 months	Infants begin to prefer familiar caregivers; build trust.
Clear-cut attachment	6/8 months – 18/24 months	Strong attachment forms: separation anxiety and protest emerge.
Formation of reciprocal relationships	18/24 months +	Child understands caregiver's comings/goings; communication improves.

Figure 2.3
Mary Ainsworth's Attachment Syles (Strange Situation)

Attachment Styles	Behavior During Separation & Reunion
Secure	Distressed when caregiver leaves; easily comforted upon return.
Insecure-Avoidant	Shows little distress; avoids caregiver upon return.
Insecure-Resistant (ambivalent)	Very distressed; seeks contact but resists comfort. Clingy and hard to soothe.
Disorganized	Confused, fearful, or contradictory behavior. Often linked to trauma or neglect.

CHAPTER 2

Belonging Wasn't Built for Me

Theme: When family shapes identity through ridicule, a child learns belonging by avoiding rejection.

Mama told me that my great grandmother, Atosi, named me "Charlietta" after my daddy. His name is "Charles," but everyone calls him Charlie. Growing up, he was always short, stocky, and smooth with his conversation. He could talk you out of a house and a home if you let him. On a good day, he wore a low cut and loved a three-piece suit with a Dobb hat. Although throughout his addiction he wore whatever he could pull together at the time. He prided himself on being able to make deals. I don't think he has ever paid the asking price for a car he wanted or anything else that he bought off the streets. At home his words landed harsh, vulgar, and final. They were usually aimed at my mama. He was always a corrector and a teacher at the same time. The younger he scolded you, the quicker he taught you a lesson. Although he didn't whip us much, his words settled just as badly.

Later in life, the name my great grandmother gave me would get butchered every time it was pronounced. In school, I always heard Charletta, Sharleeta, Sharli-etta. I hated that. It didn't matter if I pronounced that it was Charlietta—they still said what they wanted. I didn't like to repeat it. Nobody else had it. I thought it was ugly when I was younger, so I nicknamed myself Cookie. I thought I was a sweet girl, so I picked something sweet for a nickname, and it stuck. My family and friends still call me Cookie today. Once I started working, I shortened Charlietta down to Charli to make it easier for my coworkers.

At school, the mispronunciations of my name came like clockwork. Teachers would pause, squint at the roll sheet, stumble over it, and then quickly correct themselves when I spoke up. They weren't cruel—they tried—but each time it landed wrong in my stomach. The whole classroom would move on, but I stayed stuck in the echo of my own name sounding foreign. Nobody laughed, but nobody shared it with me either. It was just me, sitting in that little desk, shrinking a little smaller inside.

I grew up hating my name and wishing I had an easy name to pronounce like my mama's. Her name was common, Gwendolyn, but everybody called her "Gwen." Her name fits her perfectly. She was short and skinny. Very attractive and the nicest lady you would ever meet as long as she wasn't under the influence. She is a true caregiver in her authentic state. She took in anyone that was in need and didn't think twice about it. Everyone in our family would tell me I looked just like her. I would be pleased if they told me this. I knew she looked good.

My mama had me just two days before her birthday. We were Taurus's and she made sure I knew this about us. I was born in Delaney; these were projects in Gary, Indiana. We lived in the same housing complex from the time I came home from the hospital until we left Indiana. I only have a handful of memories from there—I was about five when we moved—but that place held a special spot in my heart. I can remember waking up to "I'll Be There" playing on the radio by the Jackson Five, with the smell of fried chicken lingering through the house. Mama would be cooking, and my siblings and I would be singing, competing to see who could hit the best singing note. My mama had the most beautiful singing voice. I loved hearing her hum a song or sing a tune. "Silly" by Deniece Williams was my favorite one. Her voice mesmerized me. I would try my best to mimic her tone.

She was gentle and always made sure you had what you needed when you were at our house, as long as she was sober and present. In this state of mind, she made sure my daddy, and her children were fed and comfortable.

On the other hand, if she was drunk, her words would sting, and oh boy, did she have a way with words! Most of the time, they were thrown at my daddy when they would have their spats back and forth. She was quick and slick mouthed. I loved how she came back with words as long as they weren't at me. I used to wish my comebacks were as precise, swift, and callous as hers were—whenever I needed them to be. The way she stood up to my daddy—I admired that since I couldn't stand the way he would treat her sometimes.

When a disco song came on the radio, Daddy would pull Mama off the couch and dance with her. They called it bopping—a synchronized two-step—and they were good.

Growing up with two older siblings and two younger ones was awkward for me. They all seemed to have rhythm, but I couldn't dance at all, so my older siblings usually left me out. They would form groups and because I couldn't get the rhythm, I couldn't be a part of it.

I didn't feel teased by the world outside the house, but I also didn't feel like I fit in anywhere. Belonging wasn't offered; it was something I watched other kids slip into naturally, like hand-me-downs that actually fit. I felt like I was always tugging at sleeves too short, shoes too big.

Sometimes I would watch the other girls at recess form circles for clapping games or skipping ropes, and I would hover near the edges pretending I didn't want to join. Truth was—I wanted in. I just didn't know how to break through that invisible wall. When you grow up being told you're too much of one thing and not enough of another, you learn to sit on the sidelines even when your legs ache to run.

I sucked my thumb, so my older siblings would call me buck toothed, and say my teeth would grow over my bottom lip. I would push my front teeth back with my thumb any time I would catch myself sucking my thumb. Although my teeth weren't sticking out of my mouth, I would use my thumb to push them back just in case they started to. I didn't break the habit of sucking my thumb until I was eighteen years of age.

My siblings claimed I looked too much like Daddy, so they teased me. And the way they talked about him—like he was something to be ashamed of—taught me that his features on my face were a liability.

I joined in on the jokes about Daddy, not because I thought they were funny, but because laughing hurt less than being left out. I didn't want to look like him, but I still longed for his attention.

Although my older siblings teased me about looking like my daddy, I honestly looked like Mama growing up. Everybody in the family said so. My siblings just liked giving me a hard time.

Sometimes it felt like Mama and Daddy would be gone for hours. My siblings might say they were gone for days. This was before I understood our parents were drug addicts. I remember the next-door neighbor, Dorothy, bringing us bologna sandwiches a couple of times when we'd been alone too long. I'd pick the peppers out of the meat, put the meat back on the bread, and eat it. I would love it if she brought the sandwiches with small specs of cheese in the ham. In Delaney Projects, neighbors could check in on you, give you spankings, and treat you like one of their own. That was normal. Dorothy may have even had her own key.

Even pickles got weaponized. Mama said, "not to eat them," but . . . my siblings went ahead anyway. Hungry and unsupervised, they demolished the whole jar. Somehow, I ended up soaked in pickle brine. The juice poured over me like guilt. I don't remember which sibling drenched me in the juice, but I do remember the story and the smell—retold over the years like a family joke. It was funny to me too. It wasn't until I got older that I looked back and realized I wasn't even conscious enough to defend myself. But that didn't stop the laughter or the blame. Mama always said she knew I didn't eat the pickles since I was only about two or three when it happened. Her guilt for being gone for so long probably spared my siblings from punishment that time.

Childhood felt like a game I didn't know the rules to—and I was always playing catch-up.

But let me be clear: I love my siblings. Even when they made me cry. Even when they made me question my place. They held me down when Mama and Daddy vanished. My older sister could flip a can of corn and a bag of rice into a feast. She still cooks like that to this day. We were bonded not by softness—but by survival. And survival creates a love that holds on even when it hurts.

As I got older, the only time I really felt like I belonged was when I was the one caring for others. Feeding a sibling, holding a cousin, protecting someone smaller than me—that's when I felt steady. Belonging wasn't about being accepted into a group. For me, it was about being needed. I didn't know it then, but I was already practicing the roles I'd carry for the rest of my life—protector, provider, caretaker.

Theory in Practice: What Was Missing

Erikson's Initiative vs. Guilt (Ages 3–6):

This stage is where children begin to assert power, explore talents, and form identity through family and peer interactions (Erikson, 1963). But when exploration leads to ridicule, guilt forms. I wasn't encouraged to explore—I was mocked for it. That shaped how I saw myself: not good enough, not welcome, not safe to try.

Freud's Phallic Stage (Ages 3–6):

This stage involves developing identification with the same-sex parent (Freud, 1961). I learned from my siblings that being like my father was shameful—so I emotionally disconnected from his image. The teasing interrupted the rivalry phase with the same sex parent (Freud, 1961). It also disrupted my ability to feel pride in my origins or understand how identity connects to family. Although I love my name now, as a child having my name connected to my father's made me feel ashamed and isolated. It also didn't help that my name was hard to pronounce.

Maslow's Hierarchy:

Belonging and Esteem. Belonging wasn't a guarantee—it was something I tried to earn (Maslow, 1943). And when jokes replaced inclusion, my self-esteem began forming around avoidance. Avoid being like Dad. Avoid being blamed. Avoid being visible. This chapter echoes what Maslow calls "social needs" left unmet—how emotional isolation becomes internal narrative.

Sibling Position and Social Roles:

Birth order theorists like Alfred Adler suggest middle children often struggle for identity and validation (Erikson, 1963). That rings true. I felt like I was the overlooked center, tasked with leadership but denied voice. I didn't know how to stand out except by standing in for someone else's role.

Lessons From the Uninvited Child

Blame doesn't always come in anger—sometimes it comes in laughter. And it takes years to realize the difference. I didn't know the words for scapegoat or emotional invisibility, but I knew what it meant to be last picked, first blamed, and always catching strays from someone else's mess.

Love isn't the absence of harm. It's what persists despite harm. That's how I explain my loyalty to my siblings and my parents. We were young, hungry, and hurting—but they were all I had, even when I didn't have myself yet.

Discussion Questions

1. How does sibling teasing impact a child's identity development?
2. How might Erikson's "initiative vs. guilt" stage appear in family dynamics like these?

3. What role does scapegoating play in shaping self-esteem?
4. How does birth order influence responsibility and emotional position in a family?
5. Reflect on a moment when love coexisted with harm. How did you navigate it?

Comparative Overview of Human Development and Attachment Theories

Figure 1.1

Sigmund Freud's Psychosexual Stages of Development

Stage	Age Range	Erogenous Zone	Developmental Descriptions
Oral	Birth – 1 year	Mouth	Sucking, biting
Anal	1 – 3 years	Anus	Toilet training
Phallic	3 – 6 years	Genital	Identity with same-sex parent
Latency	6 – 12 years	Dormant	Socialization
Genitals	12+ years	Genitals	Intimacy, reflection

Figure 1.2

Lawrence Kohlberg's Stages of Moral Development

Levels	Age Range	Stage
Pre-conventional	3 – 7 years	Obedience and Punishment
Conventional	8 – 13 years	Social Approval and Law & Order
Post-conventional	13+ years	Social Contract and Universal Ethics

Figure 1.3

Jean Piaget's Cognitive Development of Moral Development

Stage	Age Range	Developmental Descriptions
Sensorimotor	Birth–2 years	Senses and Motor Coordination
Preoperational	2–7 years	Symbolic Thinking
Concrete Operational	7–11 years	Logic with Concrete Objects
Formal Operational	11+ years	Abstract Reason

Figure 1.4

Erik Erikson Psychosocial Stages of Development

Stage	Age Range	Developmental Descriptions
Infancy	Birth–1 year	Trust vs. Mistrust
Early Childhood	1–3 years	Autonomy vs. Shame/Doubt
Preschool	3–6 years	Initiative vs. Guilt
School Age	6–12 years	Industry vs. Inferiority
Adolescent	12–18 years	Identity vs. Role Confusion
Young Adulthood	18–40 years	Intimacy vs. Isolation
Middle Adulthood	40–65 years	Generativity vs. Stagnation
Maturity	65+ years	Ego Integrity vs. Despair

Comparative Overview of Human Development and Attachment Theories

Figure 2.1
Abraham Maslow's Hierarchy of Needs

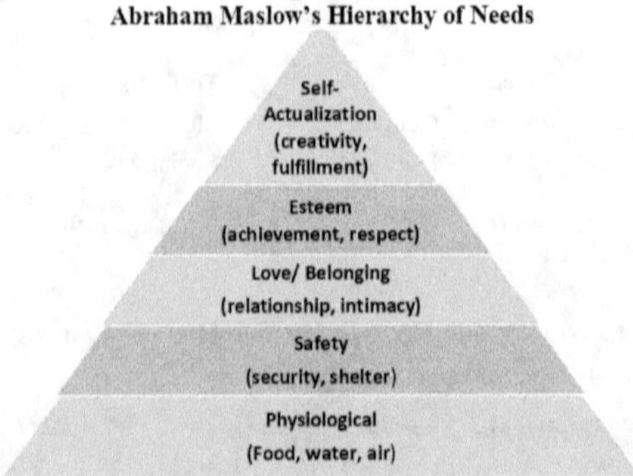

Figure 2.2
John Bowlby's Four Phases of Attachment

Phase	Age Range	Description
Pre-attachment	Birth-6 weeks	Infants show no specific attachment; respond to anyone.
Attachment-in-the-making	6 weeks - 6/8 months	Infants begin to prefer familiar caregivers; build trust.
Clear-cut attachment	6/8 months – 18/24 months	Strong attachment forms: separation anxiety and protest emerge.
Formation of reciprocal relationships	18/24 months +	Child understands caregiver's comings/goings; communication improves.

Figure 2.3
Mary Ainsworth's Attachment Syles (Strange Situation)

Attachment Styles	Behavior During Separation & Reunion
Secure	Distressed when caregiver leaves; easily comforted upon return.
Insecure-Avoidant	Shows little distress; avoids caregiver upon return.
Insecure-Resistant (ambivalent)	Very distressed; seeks contact but resists comfort. Clingy and hard to soothe.
Disorganized	Confused, fearful, or contradictory behavior. Often linked to trauma or neglect.

CHAPTER 3

Even Familiar Was Frightening

Theme: Familiarity doesn't guarantee safety—sometimes it hides the deepest harm.

I woke up next to my sister with a sawed-off shotgun lying between us. That's not something a child forgets, no matter who denies it. My father says it never happened. My mother says it did. But in my memory, that steel didn't lie. It was cold. It was real. And it was inches from our skin.

I was about six. The house was still—but not the kind of still that means peace. It was the kind that comes after chaos. I remember hearing, "Get the f*** down!" and then seeing my mother knocked out on the floor by the very drug dealers who sold them the drugs. Right before the robbery and break-in, my father had stashed guns and drugs in the push ceilings. It was like he knew what was about to happen, and they came looking.

I still hear the yelling from that house. My father's voice ricocheted through the walls like it was trying to pin us in place. The night Mama hit the floor; his command was sharp: "Get to the back room!" We ran fast, hearts pounding, trying to swallow the sight of her lying there. We didn't question—we obeyed. That order, barked over our fear, made safety sound like silence.

I don't remember how it got there. I don't know what day it was or what I was wearing. I just remember the panic merged to silence. The kind of fear that hums under your ribs without making a sound. My body knew before my brain could catch up. I remember waking up confused by the weight of the gun between us. I remember staring at the weapon, unsure if it had been used or if it was waiting to be. I didn't scream. I just watched.

Silence held me down harder than fear. When you're raised in disorder, chaos becomes predictable. Familiar. I wasn't surprised—I was trained. I was already learning how to shut down emotions before they showed up. Already learning how to stop asking questions nobody wanted to answer.

My sister remembers that night like I do. My mother confirms it. But my father refuses to speak on it. Says it never happened. He called it imagination. Misunderstanding. But my memory doesn't need his permission.

I learned something crucial that night: Familiarity doesn't mean safety. Someone can be there and still harm you. A house can be full and still feel dangerous. A father can share stories about the good old days one week and deny your truth the next. And still—this was my home.

I carried that truth alone for years. And that's the part survival never explains well: not just making it through but holding on to everything nobody else will.

That nightmare happened in the Blue House, maybe a year after we moved to Minneapolis, Minnesota. We had different family members come and stay with us at different times. Drug addicts came and went. Daddy argued with mama non-stop.

Not every memory was chaos, but even the ordinary ones carried weight. I remember my sixth birthday in that same house. My teacher had pinned a bright green four-leaf clover to my shirt with the number six in the center. I wore it all day, proud in a way I didn't often get to feel. But when I came home, the brightness of that little paper clover didn't match the heaviness inside those walls. It felt strange, almost wrong, to carry something so simple and cheerful into a place that was anything but what you would describe as joyful and safe.

There were other moments in that home that marked me too—like when my sister was hit by a company van. She came home on crutches, hobbling through the same door we ran through in fear so many times. Even her injury folded itself into the rhythm of survival. Nothing slowed down, not even pain. It was as if we were expected to keep going, no matter what the body carried.

Although Daddy was strict with his words, I only remember one good whipping from him. This was because one of my closest cousins and I picked up a cigarette butt that was still lit, which Daddy had flicked on the ground before he pulled off in his car. We decided to go to the side of the house and take some puffs.

A neighbor reported us to the grown-ups of the house after catching us. The grown-ups were my Aunty Robin and Aunty Jean. They were very strict and to the point.

They made us, at the age of six, smoke a cigarette in front of them since we thought we were grown. "Hold it in, and you better not cough," they told us. I couldn't take the smoke. I felt like my chest was caving in trying to hold the smoke in my mouth. My cousin on the other hand, who was also six at the time, held her cigarette between her fingers, blowing out a slow and smooth cloud of smoke. She smoked it like she had done this before.

When I started to take my second puff, as I was instructed to do by my aunts, my daddy walked in the door. "What the hell you doing girl?" he yelled at me. Both of my aunts interrupted his yelling, explaining to him that the neighbor had caught my cousin and me on the side of the house smoking the lit cigarette butt that he threw out his window before he pulled off.

He immediately snatched the cigarette out of my hand and yelled, "You know better than to be smoking a cigarette, get that sh*t out your mouth." He turned to me and yelled, "You get yo tail in the room, I'm whipping yo azz." He grabbed the belt and grabbed my arm. I immediately took off running on the wooden floor before he could hit me. I remember running and sliding underneath the bed in the room like I was trying to make it to second base before I was struck out. When I made it underneath the bed, I moved as far back to the wall as possible so the belt couldn't reach me.

This was a bed with metal springs on the bedframe. I remember while I was underneath the bed trying my best to stay back, one of my braids at the top of my head got caught on to one of the metal springs of the bedframe. This didn't stop him from swinging the belt.

He was furious, swearing every word in the book, telling me how bad it was that I picked up the butt of his cigarette and puffed on it. He must have swung the belt over twenty-five times but only caught me about three or four times with the tip of the belt. This was normally how he whipped us kids. He could never really catch us with the belt, or he just never really wanted to. After years, I figured this out.

He was a protector of his kids when he wanted to be and didn't care about taking a loss as long as he got his point across. He didn't back down from a soul and made sure that everybody knew it. He taught me early on that no matter how big a person is, never let them see me sweat and always stand up to them. As I got older, he showed me what part of my fist to hit with if I ever had to defend myself.

Looking back, I don't think I realized I was unsafe. I thought this was natural—watching Daddy abuse Mama, and the times my siblings and I would jump into the fight to help Mama whenever it happened. Hearing the yelling, learning to run when he told us—that was just life to me. Familiar didn't mean safe, but I didn't know the difference yet.

Theory in Practice: How This Moment Shaped Me

Maslow's Hierarchy of Needs:

Safety Replaced by Survival The lowest level—physical safety—was shattered (Maslow, 1943). Guns, violence, unconscious parents. I wasn't just lacking shelter or food; I was learning to accept threats as normal. That need for protection never got met—it got bypassed.

Freud's Psychosexual Development:

Phallic Stage Disruption Ages 3–6 is when children form identity, bodily boundaries, and emotional templates for intimacy (Freud, 1961). Exposure to violence and denial this early creates repression and confusion. I began disconnecting from my environment, not by choice—but because safety required numbness.

Erikson's Initiative vs. Guilt Stage (Ages 3–6):

This stage is about taking initiative, trying new things, asking questions (Erikson, 1963). But curiosity in my world felt dangerous. Asking what happened led to silence or shame. I didn't just learn to be quiet—I learned to feel guilty for needing clarity.

Lessons From a Silenced Memory

Truth is heavy when you're the only one holding it. That night taught me that survival meant silence. That even something terrifying—like waking up next to a weapon—could be brushed aside, denied, buried. But my memory spoke louder than their silence. And someday, I knew I'd speak it too.

Discussion Questions

1. What does denial from a caregiver teach a child about their own memory and reality?
2. How might Freud's concept of repression apply to early traumatic events like this?
3. How does Maslow's hierarchy help explain the need to normalize threat?
4. In what ways might early exposure to violence impact Erikson's initiative/guilt stage?
5. Reflect on a moment in your life when familiarity masked danger. What shifted in your thinking?

Comparative Overview of Human Development and Attachment Theories

Figure 1.1

Sigmund Freud's Psychosexual Stages of Development

Stage	Age Range	Erogenous Zone	Developmental Descriptions
Oral	Birth – 1 year	Mouth	Sucking, biting
Anal	1 – 3 years	Anus	Toilet training
Phallic	3 – 6 years	Genital	Identity with same-sex parent
Latency	6 – 12 years	Dormant	Socialization
Genitals	12+ years	Genitals	Intimacy, reflection

Figure 1.2

Lawrence Kohlberg's Stages of Moral Development

Levels	Age Range	Stage
Pre-conventional	3 – 7 years	Obedience and Punishment
Conventional	8 – 13 years	Social Approval and Law & Order
Post-conventional	13+ years	Social Contract and Universal Ethics

Figure 1.3

Jean Piaget's Cognitive Development of Moral Development

Stage	Age Range	Developmental Descriptions
Sensorimotor	Birth–2 years	Senses and Motor Coordination
Preoperational	2–7 years	Symbolic Thinking
Concrete Operational	7–11 years	Logic with Concrete Objects
Formal Operational	11+ years	Abstract Reason

Figure 1.4

Erik Erikson Psychosocial Stages of Development

Stage	Age Range	Developmental Descriptions
Infancy	Birth–1 year	Trust vs. Mistrust
Early Childhood	1–3 years	Autonomy vs. Shame/Doubt
Preschool	3–6 years	Initiative vs. Guilt
School Age	6–12 years	Industry vs. Inferiority
Adolescent	12–18 years	Identity vs. Role Confusion
Young Adulthood	18–40 years	Intimacy vs. Isolation
Middle Adulthood	40–65 years	Generativity vs. Stagnation
Maturity	65+ years	Ego Integrity vs. Despair

Comparative Overview of Human Development and Attachment Theories

Figure 2.1
Abraham Maslow's Hierarchy of Needs

Figure 2.2
John Bowlby's Four Phases of Attachment

Phase	Age Range	Description
Pre-attachment	Birth-6 weeks	Infants show no specific attachment; respond to anyone.
Attachment-in-the-making	6 weeks - 6/8 months	Infants begin to prefer familiar caregivers; build trust.
Clear-cut attachment	6/8 months – 18/24 months	Strong attachment forms: separation anxiety and protest emerge.
Formation of reciprocal relationships	18/24 months +	Child understands caregiver's comings/goings; communication improves.

Figure 2.3
Mary Ainsworth's Attachment Syles (Strange Situation)

Attachment Styles	Behavior During Separation & Reunion
Secure	Distressed when caregiver leaves; easily comforted upon return.
Insecure-Avoidant	Shows little distress; avoids caregiver upon return.
Insecure-Resistant (ambivalent)	Very distressed; seeks contact but resists comfort. Clingy and hard to soothe.
Disorganized	Confused, fearful, or contradictory behavior. Often linked to trauma or neglect.

CHAPTER 4

When Sirens Became Signal

Theme: Growing up in chaos teaches children to read danger like a second language.

We laughed at the old man's face—eyes wide, mouth open, hand clutched to his lips like he'd seen a ghost. The giggling and teasing stopped all at once. As we walked toward him, we grew curious. Mama had hurriedly told us to get to the park not even five minutes earlier. It was just another block past the man standing there, still. Something didn't look right on his face.

We figured it out too late. He wasn't looking at us—he was looking past us. I followed his gaze and turned around only to see what he saw: squad cars bleeding blue into our block. Shouting louder than church choirs. We ran back toward the house, crying, "Mama! Mama!"

That's the day we learned what a paddy wagon looked like.

We saw it circle the block twice before Mama made us leave. That's when we started keeping watch.

I was around eight. Little, but not too little to know when something was off. When the grown-ups shifted, so did we.

Safety wasn't given—it was decoded. We learned to recognize tone changes, silent stretches, and the difference between play yelling and the kind that split ceilings. My dad's continuous raging voice had volume. My mom's pain had silence. Both trained me. Both kept me alert.

When your parents vanish—whether in and out the door at all hours of the night or escaping to get away from the reality they made for us—you learn that stability is a myth. You create your own forms of control: hide in the closet, memorize the areas of the neighborhood, ask fewer questions. We weren't protected—we were perceptive. That's not the same thing, but it was all we had.

Our house was not one of emotional regulation. Feelings came and went without warning. Food did too. That's how I learned hunger had a mood. No groceries meant Mama had been gone too long and we felt empty just like the fridge, and now it was left up to big sis to figure it out. Emotions rode in the backseat of circumstance. And we were expected to buckle up and behave. And when they came back and came down off of their high, that's what we called our normal.

I didn't know I was becoming someone else—some version of myself shaped around sirens and shortages. But every time I anticipated instead of asking, every time I stayed quiet to stay safe, I was becoming her. The girl who knew how to duck but not how to feel.

That day the squad cars came, my body froze first—like fear had glued my feet to the ground. Then I bolted straight toward the police, thinking maybe they meant safety and something went wrong at home with my parents again. My siblings ran with me, all of us stuck together like magnets. If my aunt hadn't pulled up in a van right then, we probably would've been under child protection that day. I still remember the sting of watching one of my baby cousins carried out of the house. She was placed with my grandmother. Her older sister had already been removed a few weeks earlier. We were the same age and we were close, so when she was removed it felt like I lost the only person that understood everything we were going through. She was also placed with my grandmother who lived back in Gary, Indianna. Till this very day we are still close. We still complete each other's sentences. We still share most of these stories together. It was like the system circled us, one child at a time, until it closed in.

Food was just as unpredictable as the sirens. We never had much in the cupboards. My oldest sister became the cook, making her famous cheese rice—government cheese melted over white rice. That was the best meal we had, and even now I can taste it. It filled our stomachs, but more than that, it gave us a moment of comfort when comfort was scarce.

We learned to read people the way other kids read storybooks. A cousin or friend might answer back too casually, and all of us would tense up. They didn't know the rules. But we did. Mama, my aunt, or any grown-up in the house didn't have to yell—just a tight lip was enough. That tiny gesture told us everything: Straighten up, lower your eyes, stop talking. We could predict moods before they even arrived. That was survival disguised as respect.

Theory in Practice: How Safety Gets Rerouted

Erikson's Industry vs. Inferiority (Ages 6–12):

This stage asks: "Can I do things that matter?" (Erikson, 1963). But survival-mode children don't get the luxury of skill-building or self-esteem. We become good at crisis management, not creativity. When praise is rare and chaos is constant, children learn competence through coping—not confidence.

Maslow's Safety and Belonging Needs:

Safety is foundational. Without it, higher-order growth stalls (Maslow, 1943). I couldn't explore friendship or self-acceptance because my nervous system was too busy bracing. I didn't trust quiet. I didn't believe in comfort. Maslow might call that "arrested development." I call it "learned alertness."

Trauma and Hypervigilance:

Hypervigilance is the overdeveloped response to chronic threat—something trauma researchers identify as common in children who witness rage, addiction, and instability. It rewires the brain for threat detection, sometimes at the expense of joy. I didn't know how to relax because relaxing felt risky (van der Kolk, 2003).

Emotional Self-Concept Formation:

When fear shapes your foundation, identity follows (Erikson, 1963, p. 25). I started seeing myself as "the one who watches"—the responsible one, the quiet one, the fixer. But those identities weren't choices. They were reactions.

Lessons From a Siren-Tuned Childhood

The sound of safety isn't silence—it's consistency. I didn't have that. I had unpredictability dressed up in jokes, love wrapped in warnings. I became good at sensing mood shifts because that skill meant survival. But it also meant I skipped steps other kids got to take. I didn't build self-esteem or self-confidence—I built a shield.

There's power in naming this, though. There's healing in returning to the sirens and saying: I remember. I know. I adapted. And I deserve to grow beyond the sound.

Discussion Questions

1. How does chronic unpredictability affect emotional development in children?
2. What signs of hypervigilance do we often overlook in "well-behaved" kids?
3. How might a lack of safety impact a child's ability to develop self-esteem and identity?
4. What does Erikson's "industry" look like in a household focused on survival?
5. What parts of trauma often get normalized in family culture—and how can naming them shift healing?

Comparative Overview of Human Development and Attachment Theories

Figure 1.1

Sigmund Freud's Psychosexual Stages of Development

Stage	Age Range	Erogenous Zone	Developmental Descriptions
Oral	Birth – 1 year	Mouth	Sucking, biting
Anal	1 – 3 years	Anus	Toilet training
Phallic	3 – 6 years	Genital	Identity with same-sex parent
Latency	6 – 12 years	Dormant	Socialization
Genitals	12+ years	Genitals	Intimacy, reflection

Figure 1.2

Lawrence Kohlberg's Stages of Moral Development

Levels	Age Range	Stage
Pre-conventional	3 – 7 years	Obedience and Punishment
Conventional	8 – 13 years	Social Approval and Law & Order
Post-conventional	13+ years	Social Contract and Universal Ethics

Figure 1.3

Jean Piaget's Cognitive Development of Moral Development

Stage	Age Range	Developmental Descriptions
Sensorimotor	Birth–2 years	Senses and Motor Coordination
Preoperational	2–7 years	Symbolic Thinking
Concrete Operational	7–11 years	Logic with Concrete Objects
Formal Operational	11+ years	Abstract Reason

Figure 1.4

Erik Erikson Psychosocial Stages of Development

Stage	Age Range	Developmental Descriptions
Infancy	Birth–1 year	Trust vs. Mistrust
Early Childhood	1–3 years	Autonomy vs. Shame/Doubt
Preschool	3–6 years	Initiative vs. Guilt
School Age	6–12 years	Industry vs. Inferiority
Adolescent	12–18 years	Identity vs. Role Confusion
Young Adulthood	18–40 years	Intimacy vs. Isolation
Middle Adulthood	40–65 years	Generativity vs. Stagnation
Maturity	65+ years	Ego Integrity vs. Despair

Comparative Overview of Human Development and Attachment Theories

Figure 2.1
Abraham Maslow's Hierarchy of Needs

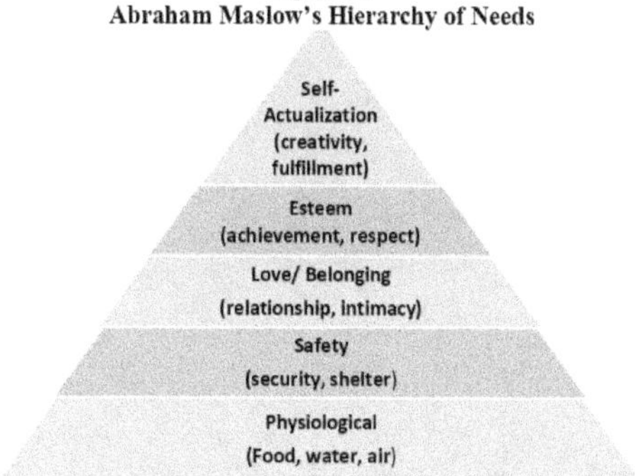

Figure 2.2
John Bowlby's Four Phases of Attachment

Phase	Age Range	Description
Pre-attachment	Birth-6 weeks	Infants show no specific attachment; respond to anyone.
Attachment-in-the-making	6 weeks - 6/8 months	Infants begin to prefer familiar caregivers; build trust.
Clear-cut attachment	6/8 months – 18/24 months	Strong attachment forms: separation anxiety and protest emerge.
Formation of reciprocal relationships	18/24 months +	Child understands caregiver's comings/goings; communication improves.

Figure 2.3
Mary Ainsworth's Attachment Syles (Strange Situation)

Attachment Styles	Behavior During Separation & Reunion
Secure	Distressed when caregiver leaves; easily comforted upon return.
Insecure-Avoidant	Shows little distress; avoids caregiver upon return.
Insecure-Resistant (ambivalent)	Very distressed; seeks contact but resists comfort. Clingy and hard to soothe.
Disorganized	Confused, fearful, or contradictory behavior. Often linked to trauma or neglect.

CHAPTER 5

Wherever We Slept, We Survived

Theme: Stability isn't defined by walls—it's measured in the rare moments where you feel safe inside them.

We slept on concrete once. Not metaphorically—literally. In an abandoned gambling joint across the street from the house that got raided. No heat. No beds. Just our bodies against the floor, stacked like worn dice. I remember shivering, not from weather, but from the kind of exposure that comes when adults stop pretending things are okay. Nobody said it aloud, but we knew there were no other options.

I can still feel the weight of that concrete on my bones. It wasn't just the cold hardness of the floor—it was the feeling that life could collapse without warning, that tomorrow had no guarantee of comfort. That night left a print on me. Even now, when I lie in a soft bed, a part of me remembers the floor. Trauma works like that—it embeds itself, not just in memory but in the body as well.

And then the shelter. Just like that. We got space, a bed, something softer than stone. I slept deeper than I ever had. Even as a child, I knew that kind of sleep wasn't normal—it was rare. It didn't last. But in that moment, it was everything.

The shelter felt like a miracle at first, but miracles can also be fragile. Beds and blankets made us feel human again, but in the back of my mind, I knew it could vanish. I learned not to get too comfortable, even in comfort. That's the quiet lesson of instability: Never let yourself believe safety is permanent. Children shouldn't have to carry that kind of wisdom, but I did.

Soon after, we moved again. A house this time. My parents were trying—really trying. But the slumlord gave us a house flooded from the inside. The main floor carpet squished underneath our feet. Water soaked the soles of my shoes—not the whole shoe, but enough to know that normal wasn't coming back anytime soon.

The flooded house was another reminder. My parents wanted so badly to make things right, and I could see their effort. But effort doesn't stop water from rising through the floors. I tiptoed across carpet that squished with every step, embarrassed by the smell, embarrassed by the truth of where we lived. Poverty is never just about not having enough—it's about having your dignity soaked out of you, piece by piece.

Then came the reporters. Bright-eyed and blank-faced, ready to turn our pain into evening news. They were there to report on the condition of the home that we had just moved into. I remember pulling the curtains tight with my siblings, standing behind the creases that our skinny little bodies fit right into, so they wouldn't see us. We didn't want to be the story. We just wanted to disappear. But silence doesn't hide water. Or shame. Or the way your body remembers sleeping on concrete even when you're standing on soaked carpet.

And the reporters? They weren't there to help. They came to capture pain, to wrap it up in a neat headline, and then move on. We didn't want pity—we wanted privacy. But when you grow up in poverty, privacy is a luxury. The curtains couldn't protect us from their curiosity, or from the world deciding what our story was before we could even speak it. That's the cruel part of being young —with no support or resources you don't get to control the narrative.

Years later, I'd learn there's a theory for all of this. Developmental psychology calls it toxic stress—the kind that doesn't just challenge you but rewires your sense of safety and your ability to trust the world (Maslow, 1943, p. 376). Social work calls it environmental trauma—the way surroundings shape outcomes before you even realize what's happening (Bowlby, 1982, p. 666). But at the time, I didn't know those words. I just knew what it meant to carry concrete sleep in my body, soggy carpet under my shoes, and shame pressed against the curtains of a broken home.

Concrete, shelters, flooded homes, and cameras—all of it formed the early blueprint of my nervous system. Theories would later confirm what I already lived: chronic instability alters development (Maslow, 1943, p. 376). Safety isn't just about walls and roofs—it's about trust, belonging, and dignity. My story is proof that what children endure in their environments becomes part of them, long before they ever sit in a classroom or across from a caseworker.

Theory in Practice: Psychological Transience

Maslow's Safety and Belonging Needs (Maslow, 1943):

Each living situation struck a different nerve. Concrete meant survival. Shelter gave a glimpse of safety. The flooded house reminded us that safety was temporary, and that even "progress" could come soaked in compromise. We never felt settled—we just kept moving.

Erikson's Industry vs. Inferiority (Ages 6–12):

Constant transitions blocked routine, structure, and growth. How do you focus on learning when you're hiding from cameras? How do you build confidence when your home feels like a liability?

Piaget's Concrete Operational Stage:

Logic and cause-effect learning were undermined by adult actions (Piaget, 1952; Huitt & Hummel, 2003). We were supposed to be mastering reasoning, but the world made no sense. Shelter came and went. Flooding became housing. News became our front porch. I started learning that logic was a luxury.

Lessons From a Cold Floor

Sometimes a bed isn't a bed—it's warmth for one night. Sometimes a home isn't a home—it's a soaked carpet you tiptoe through, pretending things are okay. And sometimes survival is hiding behind a curtain, so your poverty doesn't get broadcast. I remember those places, not for how they felt but for how they shaped me. Because wherever we slept, we kept living. And that alone was proof of something powerful.

Discussion Questions

1. How does temporary shelter impact a child's sense of stability and identity?
2. What psychological effects can come from moving rapidly between unsafe environments?
3. In what ways do children internalize public attention (like news coverage) of private hardship?

4. How does Maslow's model apply differently when "shelter" is inconsistent or stigmatized?
5. Think of a time your environment changed quickly. What did it teach you about safety and control?

Comparative Overview of Human Development and Attachment Theories

Figure 1.1

Sigmund Freud's Psychosexual Stages of Development

Stage	Age Range	Erogenous Zone	Developmental Descriptions
Oral	Birth – 1 year	Mouth	Sucking, biting
Anal	1 – 3 years	Anus	Toilet training
Phallic	3 – 6 years	Genital	Identity with same-sex parent
Latency	6 – 12 years	Dormant	Socialization
Genitals	12+ years	Genitals	Intimacy, reflection

Figure 1.2

Lawrence Kohlberg's Stages of Moral Development

Levels	Age Range	Stage
Pre-conventional	3 – 7 years	Obedience and Punishment
Conventional	8 – 13 years	Social Approval and Law & Order
Post-conventional	13+ years	Social Contract and Universal Ethics

Figure 1.3

Jean Piaget's Cognitive Development of Moral Development

Stage	Age Range	Developmental Descriptions
Sensorimotor	Birth–2 years	Senses and Motor Coordination
Preoperational	2–7 years	Symbolic Thinking
Concrete Operational	7–11 years	Logic with Concrete Objects
Formal Operational	11+ years	Abstract Reason

Figure 1.4

Erik Erikson Psychosocial Stages of Development

Stage	Age Range	Developmental Descriptions
Infancy	Birth–1 year	Trust vs. Mistrust
Early Childhood	1–3 years	Autonomy vs. Shame/Doubt
Preschool	3–6 years	Initiative vs. Guilt
School Age	6–12 years	Industry vs. Inferiority
Adolescent	12–18 years	Identity vs. Role Confusion
Young Adulthood	18–40 years	Intimacy vs. Isolation
Middle Adulthood	40–65 years	Generativity vs. Stagnation
Maturity	65+ years	Ego Integrity vs. Despair

Comparative Overview of Human Development and Attachment Theories

Figure 2.1
Abraham Maslow's Hierarchy of Needs

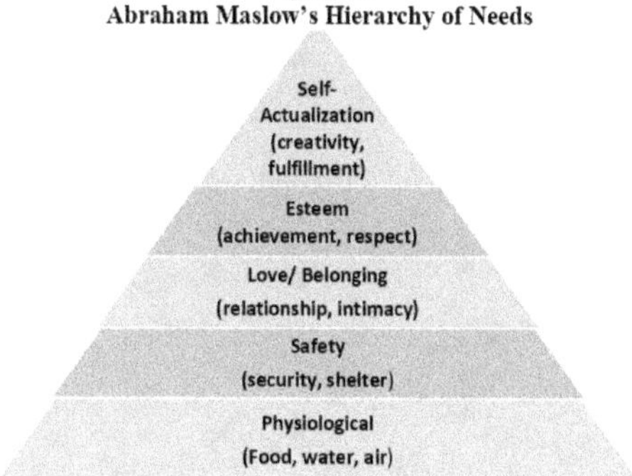

Figure 2.2
John Bowlby's Four Phases of Attachment

Phase	Age Range	Description
Pre-attachment	Birth-6 weeks	Infants show no specific attachment; respond to anyone.
Attachment-in-the-making	6 weeks - 6/8 months	Infants begin to prefer familiar caregivers; build trust.
Clear-cut attachment	6/8 months – 18/24 months	Strong attachment forms: separation anxiety and protest emerge.
Formation of reciprocal relationships	18/24 months +	Child understands caregiver's comings/goings; communication improves.

Figure 2.3
Mary Ainsworth's Attachment Syles (Strange Situation)

Attachment Styles	Behavior During Separation & Reunion
Secure	Distressed when caregiver leaves; easily comforted upon return.
Insecure-Avoidant	Shows little distress; avoids caregiver upon return.
Insecure-Resistant (ambivalent)	Very distressed; seeks contact but resists comfort. Clingy and hard to soothe.
Disorganized	Confused, fearful, or contradictory behavior. Often linked to trauma or neglect.

CHAPTER 6

Backpacks Don't Carry Trauma Well

Theme: Learning takes a backseat when survival rides in the front row.

I used to sit in class and stare at the board like it was written in fog. The teacher's voice sounded distant—underwater, almost. It wasn't that I didn't want to learn. It was that my brain couldn't make room for it.

My stomach growled through math. My mind raced through lunch. What was waiting for me at home? Would Mama be there? Would Daddy be mad again? Would they be drunk, asleep, or high?

My mind would be drifting throughout the day at school. I loved coming home to the music playing and family at the card table playing spades or dominos. I was supposed to be learning fractions, but my thoughts were already divided. One part focused on escape routes. Another on my siblings. Another on how to survive if things went left when I got back home. School couldn't compete with that.

We didn't live near the school, not really. Sometimes I'd have to walk miles home—alone, unfamiliar territory, busy highways buzzing past me like they didn't see me at all. I'd cross intersections I couldn't pronounce, guess turns, follow strangers from a distance hoping they were headed toward the direction of my house. I somehow always made it home though.

No one taught me how to get there or back, but I learned how to pay attention and spot landmarks.

Those long walks home from school scared me more than I ever admitted back then. My legs would shake, but I kept moving, teaching myself how to feel my way through unfamiliar streets. It's a skill that's stayed with me even now—trusting my instincts when I don't know the map. Usually, it was only during the first week of school that I got turned around, but the fear of getting lost always sat heavy. Somehow, I always found my way back.

At school, I learned how to seem okay. Teachers love good kids. Quiet kids. I tried. I couldn't answer questions because I barely understood them since my attention was never where it was supposed to be. I stayed seated. But inside, I was scrambled. I wasn't building knowledge—I was building defense mechanisms. I wasn't thinking about passing the spelling test—I was trying to make it through to the next hour without getting teased about my raggedy clothes, which my mama would rush me out the door in.

Clothes carried their own weight. We depended on the donation closet, picking out what we could, so at least we had something to wear. It wasn't about fashion—it was about survival. Still, kids chose to be cruel. They noticed the difference right away, and I can still hear the way their words cut—about how I dressed. I didn't have one outfit that embarrassed me most—it was all of them. Every shirt, every pair of shoes felt like a spotlight I didn't want. By the time I got to middle and high school, I made sure to overcompensate with how I dressed, because I never wanted to feel that small again.

Inside the classroom, I drifted in and out. Sometimes I was so exhausted that I just laid my head down and slept. Other times, I stared hard at the page but couldn't take in a single word. The worst was when the teacher called on me to read out loud. My chest would tighten, my hands would sweat, and the sound of my own voice felt unbearable. I'd rush through sentences, tripping on words, wishing I could disappear. I wasn't just quiet—I was watchful. I studied everything: the way kids opened their lunch boxes, the neat bows in their hair, their matching backpacks and pencil boxes. I stayed small and observed, because watching was easier than being seen.

Theory in Practice: Why School Doesn't Always Save

Maslow's Hierarchy—Physiological and Safety Needs Unmet:

Basic needs—food, shelter, security—weren't consistent. My body was always in fight-or-flight. That doesn't leave room for focus, memory, or joy in learning. Maslow's model makes it clear that without those foundational needs, motivation and learning falter (Maslow, 1943).

Erikson's Industry vs. Inferiority (Ages 6–12):

This stage depends on feedback, encouragement, and routine (Erikson, 1963). But when external chaos rules, children feel incapable, disconnected, less-than. I started believing I wasn't smart—not because I lacked ability but because I lacked the emotional bandwidth.

Cognitive Load Theory:

Psychologists explain that when a child's working memory is overloaded by stress, learning stalls (Piaget, 1952; Huitt & Hummel, 2003). I was trying to process trauma while decoding long division. That's not equal footing—it's impossible terrain.

Attachment Disruption and Educational Gaps:

Consistent care leads to confidence (Bowlby, 1982; Bretherton, 1992). Without it, children hesitate to ask questions, take risks, or seek help. I didn't ask—I just tried to vanish behind my desk and wait for dismissal.

Lessons From a Sidewalk Scholar

Being a student while being unsafe is like asking a drowning child to recite spelling words. I learned to navigate city streets before I learned to write in cursive. I became emotionally fluent before I learned grammar.

School wasn't a failure—it just wasn't enough. And that taught me to stop blaming myself for not being able to focus. Because when your world feels unstable, attention is a luxury you don't own.

Discussion Questions

1. What does Maslow's hierarchy tell us about why some children struggle in school?
2. How can chronic stress impact cognitive processing and academic performance?
3. Why might a quiet or compliant child still be emotionally overwhelmed?

4. How does Erikson’s industry/inferiority stage show up in classroom behaviors?
5. Reflect on a moment when you had to perform “okay” when you weren’t. What did it cost you?

Comparative Overview of Human Development and Attachment Theories

Figure 1.1

Sigmund Freud's Psychosexual Stages of Development

Stage	Age Range	Erogenous Zone	Developmental Descriptions
Oral	Birth – 1 year	Mouth	Sucking, biting
Anal	1 – 3 years	Anus	Toilet training
Phallic	3 – 6 years	Genital	Identity with same-sex parent
Latency	6 – 12 years	Dormant	Socialization
Genitals	12+ years	Genitals	Intimacy, reflection

Figure 1.2

Lawrence Kohlberg's Stages of Moral Development

Levels	Age Range	Stage
Pre-conventional	3 – 7 years	Obedience and Punishment
Conventional	8 – 13 years	Social Approval and Law & Order
Post-conventional	13+ years	Social Contract and Universal Ethics

Figure 1.3

Jean Piaget's Cognitive Development of Moral Development

Stage	Age Range	Developmental Descriptions
Sensorimotor	Birth–2 years	Senses and Motor Coordination
Preoperational	2–7 years	Symbolic Thinking
Concrete Operational	7–11 years	Logic with Concrete Objects
Formal Operational	11+ years	Abstract Reason

Figure 1.4

Erik Erikson Psychosocial Stages of Development

Stage	Age Range	Developmental Descriptions
Infancy	Birth–1 year	Trust vs. Mistrust
Early Childhood	1–3 years	Autonomy vs. Shame/Doubt
Preschool	3–6 years	Initiative vs. Guilt
School Age	6–12 years	Industry vs. Inferiority
Adolescent	12–18 years	Identity vs. Role Confusion
Young Adulthood	18–40 years	Intimacy vs. Isolation
Middle Adulthood	40–65 years	Generativity vs. Stagnation
Maturity	65+ years	Ego Integrity vs. Despair

Comparative Overview
of Human Development and Attachment Theories

Figure 2.1
Abraham Maslow's Hierarchy of Needs

Figure 2.2
John Bowlby's Four Phases of Attachment

Phase	Age Range	Description
Pre-attachment	Birth-6 weeks	Infants show no specific attachment; respond to anyone.
Attachment-in-the-making	6 weeks - 6/8 months	Infants begin to prefer familiar caregivers; build trust.
Clear-cut attachment	6/8 months – 18/24 months	Strong attachment forms: separation anxiety and protest emerge.
Formation of reciprocal relationships	18/24 months +	Child understands caregiver's comings/goings; communication improves.

Figure 2.3
Mary Ainsworth's Attachment Syles (Strange Situation)

Attachment Styles	Behavior During Separation & Reunion
Secure	Distressed when caregiver leaves; easily comforted upon return.
Insecure-Avoidant	Shows little distress; avoids caregiver upon return.
Insecure-Resistant (ambivalent)	Very distressed; seeks contact but resists comfort. Clingy and hard to soothe.
Disorganized	Confused, fearful, or contradictory behavior. Often linked to trauma or neglect.

CHAPTER 7

Hide and Seek Wasn't a Game

Theme: Protection, trauma, and silence—when childhood becomes a battlefield.

I was no older than nine or ten, but I knew how to build a wall. Not of bricks—but of limbs. My arm curved around their bodies like a lock. My eyes never closed until theirs did. That was the only part of me I could give away and still keep them safe.

My two younger siblings needed protection more than anything, and I made sure they had it. Mama and Daddy would fight and make up—arguments, slammed doors, long silences. Chaos became our home's soundtrack.

Then came the rupture. For the first time, Mama and Daddy split up. And in the gaps of that break, it didn't stop strangers from filling the house. Drug dealers mostly. They were allowed to sell out of our home as long as they gave up the drugs for free. Our rooms weren't ours anymore—they were theirs.

I saw my mama get stabbed by one of them. I don't know what she owed him—money, drugs, something—but I remember holding my breath and my pain in. She didn't flinch. She didn't cry. She was tough about it. So I followed suit. I wore her tough skin like armor, hoping it would mask the fear and the ache inside me.

Me and my siblings slept on the living room floor, gathering whatever pillows and covers we could find. Rough hands and heavy footsteps moved through the house all night. One of those hands found me under the covers. I knew then—I had to keep my little sister and brother safe at all times. I watched them like a hawk.

It started off once in a while. Then every other night. Then came the game: "Let's play hide-and-seek," he said. He found the closet. Found me. I said no. He kept trying. I screamed, and he ran—but the damage had already carved itself into me.

I learned to stay still, to stay silent. Most of the time, I just let it happen. My body froze even when my mind screamed no. But that night was the scariest—I couldn't stay still. His presence felt dark. My body didn't think; it moved. I shot up and ran across the street, pounding on that door with everything I had. I didn't look back. That was the first time instinct drowned out fear.

Mama was across the street getting high with my Aunty Jean. I ran to them. We would usually get a good beaten to the butt and screamed at by my aunty for interrupting them, but I didn't care about the yelling or the heavy hands this time. I banged on the door with everything I had, tears pouring down my face. My aunt opened it, already yelling, "Why the hell are you banging at my door?"

But I was already screaming, "He pulled my pants down! He touched me! He keeps touching me!"

Mama ran to the door. "Who?" she shouted. I told her. She grabbed something from the table and ran. My aunt followed.

They moved so fast I could barely keep up. By the time I got back across the street, I saw blood. Glass bottles. Knives. Swinging hands. My mama and my aunt were on him. He ran out of the house, bloody and broken.

He eventually went to prison—for assaulting other girls.

When Mama and my aunt fought him off, I felt something I hadn't felt before—relief. For once, the danger was on the outside, bleeding and broken. For once, I felt a little safer. But he wasn't the only one. There were others. And for those, I stayed silent. Silence became its own survival strategy.

I carried that silence with me for years. It wasn't until adulthood, sitting in therapy, that I found the words to speak it out loud. By then, the fear had settled so deep that it felt like a part of me. I thought keeping quiet was the only way to survive. But that night with him was different. He was the one who terrified me the most, and my body wouldn't let me stay still. I ran, I screamed, I told. That was the first time I thought that speaking out could actually stop the danger, even if only for a moment. It didn't erase everything else that happened, but it gave me proof that my voice had power. I carried that memory with me, even through years of silence, because it showed me what protection could look like when someone finally listened. This didn't last long because no one believed it when my sister told her story. They said it was her fault; I guess because she got into trouble all the time. I found out quickly that speaking up could be worse than staying silent.

A couple of days later, I was sobbing in my mama's bed. Whispering prayers into the pillow. Pleading with God. I prayed with my whole body. I just wanted somebody to save me. To save us—my siblings, my aunts, and my family. To save my parents. I wished that we had gotten taken and put into a foster home. I just wanted better than we had at the time.

That same aunt who had just stood up for me walked past my mama's room and stopped in her tracks; she saw me crying and praying. She was more than likely high. Far from herself. She told me to shut up; in a voice you just don't question. Her slaps were too loud to gamble with.

So, I did. I shut up. Immediately.

Theory in Practice: When Silence Becomes Survival

Freud's Identification Defense Mechanism:

I didn't just survive—I adapted by becoming what I thought looked strong (Freud, 1961). Freud called it identification: when a child internalizes traits of a powerful figure to cope. I wore my mama's toughness like armor, not because I felt strong—but because I couldn't afford to feel weak.

Attachment Theory—Protection and Betrayal:

When Mama and my aunt ran toward the danger, I felt seen. Protected. That moment cracked open a possibility I hadn't known before—that adults could fight for me. But when that same aunt later snapped at me for crying, the safety net unraveled. Attachment theory explains how inconsistent caregiving creates confusion: love and harm braided together (Bowlby, 1982; Bretherton, 1992). I learned to trust—but only temporarily.

Erikson's Industry vs. Inferiority (Ages 6–12):

This stage is about building competence and confidence (Erikson, 1963). But when your role becomes protector instead of learner, identity gets distorted. I wasn't inferior—I was injured. And I had no tools to name it.

Freud's Defense Mechanisms:

Repression and Suppression. I buried the trauma to keep functioning (Freud, 1961). My silence wasn't weakness—it was strategy. Freud might call it repression. I call it survival.

Resilience Theory—Adversity Meets Adaptive Strength:

Despite harm, I found a role: protector (Maslow, 1943). That's what saved me. Building meaning out of trauma didn't erase it—but it gave me a reason to stay connected. My siblings were my reason.

Lessons From Behind the Wall

What happens when a child becomes the shield instead of the protected?

When no adult listens, and no safe place exists, children build internal refugees.

Mine was made of caution and silence. Of prayers and locked limbs.

I didn't get to be a kid. I got to be the guard.

That shouldn't be normal—but it was. And it still is for far too many children.

Discussion Questions

1. How do children adapt psychologically to repeated violations of safety?
2. What role do defense mechanisms play in trauma survival?
3. Why might a child stay silent after an assault?

4. How can caregivers unintentionally reinforce trauma responses?
5. Reflect on the language of survival used in this chapter. What metaphors stand out and why?

Comparative Overview of Human Development and Attachment Theories

Figure 1.1

Sigmund Freud's Psychosexual Stages of Development

Stage	Age Range	Erogenous Zone	Developmental Descriptions
Oral	Birth – 1 year	Mouth	Sucking, biting
Anal	1 – 3 years	Anus	Toilet training
Phallic	3 – 6 years	Genital	Identity with same-sex parent
Latency	6 – 12 years	Dormant	Socialization
Genitals	12+ years	Genitals	Intimacy, reflection

Figure 1.2

Lawrence Kohlberg's Stages of Moral Development

Levels	Age Range	Stage
Pre-conventional	3 – 7 years	Obedience and Punishment
Conventional	8 – 13 years	Social Approval and Law & Order
Post-conventional	13+ years	Social Contract and Universal Ethics

Figure 1.3

Jean Piaget's Cognitive Development of Moral Development

Stage	Age Range	Developmental Descriptions
Sensorimotor	Birth–2 years	Senses and Motor Coordination
Preoperational	2–7 years	Symbolic Thinking
Concrete Operational	7–11 years	Logic with Concrete Objects
Formal Operational	11+ years	Abstract Reason

Figure 1.4

Erik Erikson Psychosocial Stages of Development

Stage	Age Range	Developmental Descriptions
Infancy	Birth–1 year	Trust vs. Mistrust
Early Childhood	1–3 years	Autonomy vs. Shame/Doubt
Preschool	3–6 years	Initiative vs. Guilt
School Age	6–12 years	Industry vs. Inferiority
Adolescent	12–18 years	Identity vs. Role Confusion
Young Adulthood	18–40 years	Intimacy vs. Isolation
Middle Adulthood	40–65 years	Generativity vs. Stagnation
Maturity	65+ years	Ego Integrity vs. Despair

Comparative Overview of Human Development and Attachment Theories

Figure 2.1
Abraham Maslow's Hierarchy of Needs

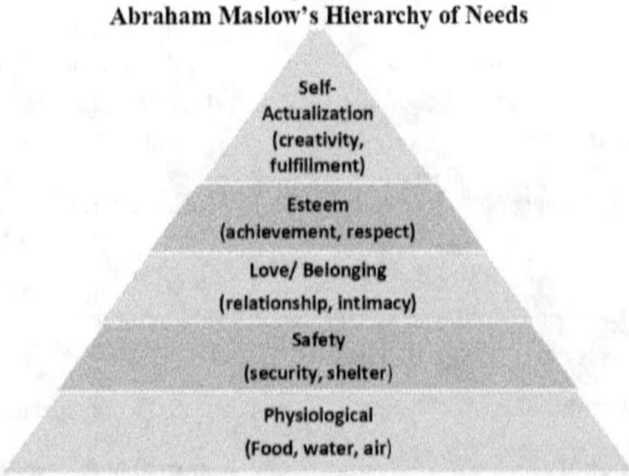

Figure 2.2
John Bowlby's Four Phases of Attachment

Phase	Age Range	Description
Pre-attachment	Birth-6 weeks	Infants show no specific attachment; respond to anyone.
Attachment-in-the-making	6 weeks - 6/8 months	Infants begin to prefer familiar caregivers; build trust.
Clear-cut attachment	6/8 months – 18/24 months	Strong attachment forms: separation anxiety and protest emerge.
Formation of reciprocal relationships	18/24 months +	Child understands caregiver's comings/goings; communication improves.

Figure 2.3
Mary Ainsworth's Attachment Syles (Strange Situation)

Attachment Styles	Behavior During Separation & Reunion
Secure	Distressed when caregiver leaves; easily comforted upon return.
Insecure-Avoidant	Shows little distress; avoids caregiver upon return.
Insecure-Resistant (ambivalent)	Very distressed; seeks contact but resists comfort. Clingy and hard to soothe.
Disorganized	Confused, fearful, or contradictory behavior. Often linked to trauma or neglect.

CHAPTER 8

The Rice, the Fire, the Stand

Theme: Sometimes protection shows up late—but it still changes everything.

I was around eleven, and all we had in that kitchen cabinet was rice. Nothing to go with it—just the kind that came in a bag with no label. I dug out a pot, ran cold water over the grains, and lit the burner on low, hoping it wouldn't burn before I got back. The kitchen smelled like old grease and wood that hadn't seen polish in years. The floor tiles were cracked, some pieces missing. But that day, I didn't care—I had somewhere to be.

My Aunty Robin, my mom's other younger sister, had just moved around the corner. North Minneapolis had been our neck of the woods since we had moved from Gary, Indianna. I knew my way good around the neighborhood by then. We moved around so much from house to house that I had each part of the Northside memorized from roaming around the neighborhood with my siblings. Mama and Daddy didn't have a car, so we walked everywhere. Mostly to the food shelves, county offices, and to get free dinner at the church or whatever hall was serving the community. So, when I left out the door of my house after throwing that pot of rice on the stove, I knew exactly where I needed to go.

Aunty Robin had her kids back. She wasn't involved in drugs anymore. During the time she was working on getting her kids back, she would come and get me to babysit. At that time, she worked at One Potato Two, a fast-food restaurant in the City Center downtown.

When I walked in, her house smelled like Pine-Sol and bleach. Her floors had plastic runners that squeaked when you walked on them with your shoes, the kind with the spikes on the other side of them. It felt familiar and comfortable compared to home. I hadn't seen her in a minute, and I couldn't wait to hug her, hear her voice, and play with my cousins. I got lost in the fun and conversation, and the rice that I had put on the stove before I left home was far from my mind at this time.

About thirty minutes in, my daddy came through her door like a thunderclap.

"You almost burned the house down!" he yelled, eyes wide, arms moving fast. He didn't knock. Didn't soften. Just stormed in and aimed the whole fire at me. He told me to get my azz back home and clean up the mess. His voice was sharp enough to slice through pride. I shrunk instinctively, my body remembering too many angry sharp yells before this one.

And then my aunt stood up. "She don't have to leave," she said, voice steady. "And you ain't gonna yell at her in my house. If she wanna stay, she's staying." The room went still.

No one had ever defended me like that. Not in front of other adults. Not like they meant it. Not without making me feel little afterward like my other aunty had made me feel when I was praying. This aunt didn't ask questions or look for proof. She saw me. She spoke. She shifted the power.

Daddy backed down that day. He didn't argue, didn't fight—he just left. I think he saw something in my aunt that shook him. She had beat an addiction that had him in a choke-hold, and maybe at that moment he knew she could beat him too. At least that's how I felt.

The difference between her house and mine was sharp. My house wasn't cold, but it felt cold—skeptical, dry, patched together as best as possible. At her house, it was alive. Kids running, music playing, cousins laughing, and that warm smell of Pine-Sol telling you someone cared enough to keep it clean. I trusted her. I had been scared of her once—her whippings were the worst. But by then, something had softened in her. She was still strict, but the sharpness was wrapped in love.

That day taught me that protection wasn't always silent. It could be loud, it could stand in the doorway, and it could change the way a child felt about herself.

This was a time when I felt protected without having to give up my safety.

She wore that protection like perfume—it lingered in the air after the argument ended. I remember sitting on her couch with a paper plate on my lap, eating hot dogs and chips with my cousins, feeling something soft inside my chest. Maybe relief. Maybe worth.

That stand didn't fix everything. But it planted something. A belief that maybe, just maybe, protection could be loud too—not just what I gave my siblings in silence. It could show up and speak up.

It wasn't the first time she had stepped in. Once, during her treatment at Turning Point, she stopped by while Mama and Daddy were fighting. She jumped in, and she and Mama gave him a beating that time. I remember screaming "Get off my daddy!" even though I was furious at him for putting his hands on my mama. I didn't know how to untangle that kind of anger and loyalty.

Later, she walked me down to the bus stop at the corner. She told me about how she was getting her kids back, how she was changing, how she was determined to stay clean. I believed her.

Theory in Practice: What That Moment Meant

Maslow's Safety and Esteem Needs:

Until then, safety was something I built by staying small, quiet, and useful. My aunt offered protection without requiring performance. That met both Maslow's safety and esteem levels—showing me I deserved care and respect (Maslow, 1943).

Erikson's Industry vs. Inferiority (Ages 6–12):

Her defense affirmed my value (Erikson, 1963). In Erikson's model, children begin developing pride through accomplishment and external affirmation. That moment told me I was worthy—not just responsible but worth defending.

Social Learning Theory:

Watching my aunt transform—recovery, reunification, boundary-setting—taught me what resilience could look like in full color (Freud, 1961). She wasn't just surviving; she was mothering, modeling, and mentoring without even trying.

Lessons From a Pot of Rice

Sometimes you don't know what protection feels like until someone hands it to you. My aunt didn't wrap me in a hug or whisper reassurances. She spoke with steel. And sometimes, that's what love sounds like.

That moment stays with me. Not just because she stood up to my daddy—but because she stood up for me. And in a childhood built on invisibility, that was a breakthrough.

Discussion Questions

1. How can public protection restore a child's sense of self-worth?
2. Why does Maslow's model suggest esteem must follow safety?
3. What lessons can children learn from witnessing adult recovery?
4. How does boundary-setting by caregivers impact emotional development?
5. Reflect on a moment when someone saw you clearly. What changed after that?

Comparative Overview of Human Development and Attachment Theories

Figure 1.1

Sigmund Freud's Psychosexual Stages of Development

Stage	Age Range	Erogenous Zone	Developmental Descriptions
Oral	Birth – 1 year	Mouth	Sucking, biting
Anal	1 – 3 years	Anus	Toilet training
Phallic	3 – 6 years	Genital	Identity with same-sex parent
Latency	6 – 12 years	Dormant	Socialization
Genitals	12+ years	Genitals	Intimacy, reflection

Figure 1.2

Lawrence Kohlberg's Stages of Moral Development

Levels	Age Range	Stage
Pre-conventional	3 – 7 years	Obedience and Punishment
Conventional	8 – 13 years	Social Approval and Law & Order
Post-conventional	13+ years	Social Contract and Universal Ethics

Figure 1.3

Jean Piaget's Cognitive Development of Moral Development

Stage	Age Range	Developmental Descriptions
Sensorimotor	Birth–2 years	Senses and Motor Coordination
Preoperational	2–7 years	Symbolic Thinking
Concrete Operational	7–11 years	Logic with Concrete Objects
Formal Operational	11+ years	Abstract Reason

Figure 1.4

Erik Erikson Psychosocial Stages of Development

Stage	Age Range	Developmental Descriptions
Infancy	Birth–1 year	Trust vs. Mistrust
Early Childhood	1–3 years	Autonomy vs. Shame/Doubt
Preschool	3–6 years	Initiative vs. Guilt
School Age	6–12 years	Industry vs. Inferiority
Adolescent	12–18 years	Identity vs. Role Confusion
Young Adulthood	18–40 years	Intimacy vs. Isolation
Middle Adulthood	40–65 years	Generativity vs. Stagnation
Maturity	65+ years	Ego Integrity vs. Despair

Comparative Overview
of Human Development and Attachment Theories

Figure 2.1
Abraham Maslow's Hierarchy of Needs

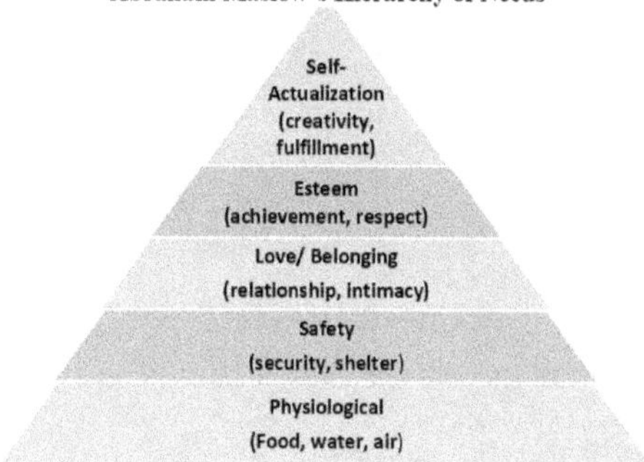

Figure 2.2
John Bowlby's Four Phases of Attachment

Phase	Age Range	Description
Pre-attachment	Birth-6 weeks	Infants show no specific attachment; respond to anyone.
Attachment-in-the-making	6 weeks - 6/8 months	Infants begin to prefer familiar caregivers; build trust.
Clear-cut attachment	6/8 months – 18/24 months	Strong attachment forms: separation anxiety and protest emerge.
Formation of reciprocal relationships	18/24 months +	Child understands caregiver's comings/goings; communication improves.

Figure 2.3
Mary Ainsworth's Attachment Syles (Strange Situation)

Attachment Styles	Behavior During Separation & Reunion
Secure	Distressed when caregiver leaves; easily comforted upon return.
Insecure-Avoidant	Shows little distress; avoids caregiver upon return.
Insecure-Resistant (ambivalent)	Very distressed; seeks contact but resists comfort. Clingy and hard to soothe.
Disorganized	Confused, fearful, or contradictory behavior. Often linked to trauma or neglect.

CHAPTER 9

Angel in the Hallway

Theme: Sometimes survival chooses the best available option—even if it's not the right one.

By the time I was in the 5th grade, the house we called home belonged to my Aunty Robin—and, by all accounts, an angel on assignment. CPS had placed custody of us in her hands: my oldest sister, my two younger siblings, and me. The sister between me and my oldest had gone to live with our grandmother. It was a split we barely understood.

We still lived in North Minneapolis, where gun violence, drugs, homelessness, and gangs were everywhere and more than likely what headlined the evening news. It was normal for us since it's all we knew growing up. We knew what to watch out for so we wouldn't get caught in the crossfire.

It wasn't perfect with my aunt. There were loud mornings and crowded bedrooms, the smell of fried bologna drifting through the hallway, homework done at sticky kitchen tables. But it was better than living in the drug houses we had been in. It was so much better. I felt safe. Protected. Seen. My cousins became siblings—lines blurred by closeness and care.

It was so easy for us to get into neighborhood fights and boy, did we get into lots of them. Aunty Robin had seven kids of her own; she also took care of four of my mother's children, and eventually she took in five of my Aunty Jean's children that she has. All together there were sixteen of us that she took care of for years. Besides my oldest sister and Aunty Robin's oldest son, I was the oldest of everyone else. Eventually some of our older cousins and their kids would move in as well. We had a large family.

I always felt like I needed to protect my younger siblings from anyone causing them any harm. This is why I got into some serious fights with other people, along with all the built-up anger from my past experiences. I couldn't stand up for myself when I was younger, so I made sure I stood up for them while we were growing up. I carried this behavior and attitude on to high school and early adulthood.

When my cousins/siblings were in foster care, even at a young age, I went out looking for them. And what's ironic is—I found them. They happened to be placed a few blocks away from where we stayed around the time our house got raided. Right across from the school that handed out free bags of lunch during the summertime. I would sneak and go see them all the time after I found out where they lived. I swore I would always come to see them. Even before they went to foster care, we lived together. So, when my aunt received custody of us, it was easy transitioning from cousins to siblings.

My aunt was stiff, sharp-tongued, and quick with her hands on your butt or in the kitchen. Her house smelled like heat and fried pork chops, like correction and comfort trying to cohabitate. The floors squeaked but her rules didn't. Shoes off. Speak clearly. Say "Yes, ma'am" whether you meant it or not.

My aunt remarried when I was about fourteen. The rhythms of the household changed—not overnight but enough that we felt the shift in the walls. Then, out of nowhere, CPS came again. This time, they removed us.

They said it was overcrowded. Or something about paperwork. No one explained clearly. All I knew was that the kitchen where I learned to stir grits was no longer mine. They took us to a foster home that looked good on paper but felt like a trap wrapped in wallpaper. The woman there wore a mask of kindness—one of those smiles that didn't reach her eyes. I knew it from day one: This wasn't safety; it was performance.

I kept trying to stay at my aunt's. The first time I ran, I took my younger siblings with me. The next time, they were too afraid to go. I ran away until even the foster provider allowed me to reside with my aunt. I just kept checking on my siblings every chance I could.

During the time with my aunt, we ended up living with a family friend—and I found myself trying to run away from the same type of sick offenses a young girl should never have to experience. Even if it was just looks that turned into fondling. It was enough to make me leave.

So, I made a choice no child should have to make: I went back to my parents. Not because it was safe but because it was familiar. I knew where the danger lay. I knew the walls. I knew how to disappear in plain sight.

Eventually, CPS let my younger siblings move back with my mama and daddy. Despite their ongoing drug use, Mama and Daddy showed the system what they needed to, and they deemed it acceptable. I wasn't okay with it. I was back in the same old environment. To make things worse, the room that was supposed to be mine was being rented to a drug dealer.

The shifts between homes, between guardians, between versions of "safety" carved something in me I didn't fully recognize until years later. Every move felt like starting over—not just with bedrooms or schools but with my sense of self. At my aunt's place, I was a protector. At the foster home, I was a runaway. Back with my parents, I was a survivor trying to outwit the chaos. Each label wasn't chosen—it was assigned. And yet I carried them all.

That's the thing about survival: You learn to measure safety not by how healthy a space is, but by how well you know its dangers. With my parents, I knew the rules of dysfunction. I could predict the patterns, sense the danger before it exploded. In strange homes, I couldn't. Familiar pain felt safer than new threats. That's a lesson no child should ever have to learn, but it was my reality.

I also think about the size of our family at my aunt's house. Sixteen kids in one house—cousins, siblings, nieces, nephews—all stacked together like a small army. Crowded? Yes. Loud? Absolutely. But within that chaos was belonging. Even with CPS looking at us like a file of numbers, inside those walls we knew who we belonged to. That belonging is what kept me running back, what made me fight to stay connected no matter what home they placed us in.

And then there's the anger. It showed up in fists, in fights, in words I didn't mean. But beneath it was a deep sense of responsibility. I couldn't save myself when I was younger, so I fought harder to shield the ones who came after me. That protective instinct is part of what shaped me into who I am today. It was a survival strategy, yes, but it also planted the seeds of advocacy.

Years later, when I studied trauma theory, I could finally name what I lived: ambiguous loss. Losing safety without losing people. Losing home without losing family. It's the kind of grief that doesn't get a funeral, but it marks you all the same. And the constant back-and-forth between caregivers? That's instability at its core—the very thing research shows alters attachment, trust, and even brain development. I didn't need a textbook to prove it. My life was the evidence.

Living between homes taught me something that theory later confirmed: Children learn to adapt even when the adaptation costs them pieces of themselves. Safety, in environments like mine, wasn't about freedom—it was about familiarity. And while systems measured overcrowding and paperwork, I was measuring where my siblings slept, who had eyes on us, and whether I could keep them safe. This is where practice and theory collide: survival becomes strategy, and strategy becomes identity. That's what it means to grow up in the hallway between safety and danger—learning to carry both.

Theory in Practice: Navigating Unseen Wounds

Erikson's Identity vs. Role Confusion (ages 12–18):

At a stage when identity formation depends on consistency, I was a revolving door of environments—each demanding a new version of me (Erikson, 1963). I wasn't developing identity; I was performing survival.

Maslow's Hierarchy—Revisiting Safety:

A locked door means nothing if what's inside violates trust (Maslow, 1943). I learned that "safety" was not a location—it was a feeling, and I rarely felt it.

Trauma-Informed Attachment Theory:

My strongest bond was with my aunt's version of home—organized, firm, loving without begging for it (Bowlby, 1982; Bretherton, 1992). When taken from that, my attachment refused substitutes. That's why I kept returning. Because love can be place-specific, and trauma doesn't transfer quietly.

Lessons From a Fractured Map

I didn't choose the safest place—I chose the one where I understood the rules, even if they cut me. Familiar pain felt less sharp than new betrayal. That's what survival does—it teaches you to stop seeking perfection and settle for predictability.

My aunt didn't save me from everything, but she gave me a memory to chase. When people talk about angels, I think of her. Not floating in white robes—but standing in house shoes, yelling down the hallway, making sure dinner got on the table.

Discussion Questions

1. How does repeated relocation affect a child's sense of self and stability?
2. What happens when "safe" adults become sources of trauma?
3. In what ways can chosen family offer better protection than biological ties?
4. Why might a child choose familiar harm over unfamiliar promise?

5. Reflect on a time when leaving wasn’t an option, and you had to adapt. What did you learn?
6. How do systems define “acceptable” parenting, and what gets lost in that definition?

Comparative Overview of Human Development and Attachment Theories

Figure 1.1

Sigmund Freud's Psychosexual Stages of Development

Stage	Age Range	Erogenous Zone	Developmental Descriptions
Oral	Birth – 1 year	Mouth	Sucking, biting
Anal	1 – 3 years	Anus	Toilet training
Phallic	3 – 6 years	Genital	Identity with same-sex parent
Latency	6 – 12 years	Dormant	Socialization
Genitals	12+ years	Genitals	Intimacy, reflection

Figure 1.2

Lawrence Kohlberg's Stages of Moral Development

Levels	Age Range	Stage
Pre-conventional	3 – 7 years	Obedience and Punishment
Conventional	8 – 13 years	Social Approval and Law & Order
Post-conventional	13+ years	Social Contract and Universal Ethics

Figure 1.3

Jean Piaget's Cognitive Development of Moral Development

Stage	Age Range	Developmental Descriptions
Sensorimotor	Birth–2 years	Senses and Motor Coordination
Preoperational	2–7 years	Symbolic Thinking
Concrete Operational	7–11 years	Logic with Concrete Objects
Formal Operational	11+ years	Abstract Reason

Figure 1.4

Erik Erikson Psychosocial Stages of Development

Stage	Age Range	Developmental Descriptions
Infancy	Birth–1 year	Trust vs. Mistrust
Early Childhood	1–3 years	Autonomy vs. Shame/Doubt
Preschool	3–6 years	Initiative vs. Guilt
School Age	6–12 years	Industry vs. Inferiority
Adolescent	12–18 years	Identity vs. Role Confusion
Young Adulthood	18–40 years	Intimacy vs. Isolation
Middle Adulthood	40–65 years	Generativity vs. Stagnation
Maturity	65+ years	Ego Integrity vs. Despair

Comparative Overview
of Human Development and Attachment Theories

Figure 2.1
Abraham Maslow's Hierarchy of Needs

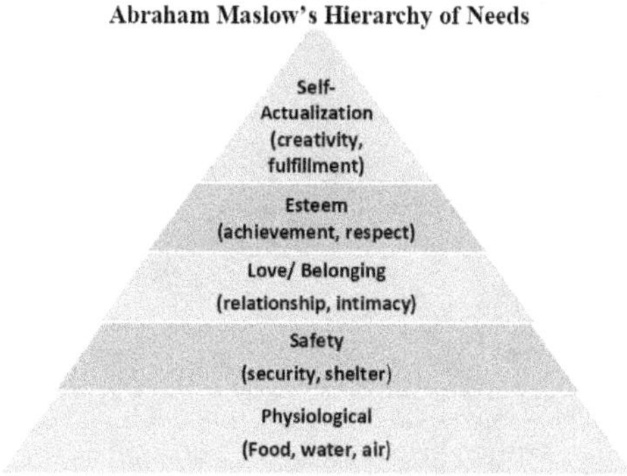

Figure 2.2
John Bowlby's Four Phases of Attachment

Phase	Age Range	Description
Pre-attachment	Birth-6 weeks	Infants show no specific attachment; respond to anyone.
Attachment-in-the-making	6 weeks - 6/8 months	Infants begin to prefer familiar caregivers; build trust.
Clear-cut attachment	6/8 months – 18/24 months	Strong attachment forms: separation anxiety and protest emerge.
Formation of reciprocal relationships	18/24 months +	Child understands caregiver's comings/goings; communication improves.

Figure 2.3
Mary Ainsworth's Attachment Syles (Strange Situation)

Attachment Styles	Behavior During Separation & Reunion
Secure	Distressed when caregiver leaves; easily comforted upon return.
Insecure-Avoidant	Shows little distress; avoids caregiver upon return.
Insecure-Resistant (ambivalent)	Very distressed; seeks contact but resists comfort. Clingy and hard to soothe.
Disorganized	Confused, fearful, or contradictory behavior. Often linked to trauma or neglect.

10

The Door Wasn't Locked

Theme: You don't always get a childhood, but you still find ways to mother.

By fourteen, I had shuffled myself out of my parents' home and into a new rhythm with my best friend and her mom. Their apartment smelled like cocoa butter and air freshener—the kind with fake ocean scents that clung to furniture legs. It wasn't mine, but it gave me peace.

I checked on my younger siblings constantly. I asked them quiet questions about what was going on. Took note of bruises that weren't quite physical. The ones that don't fade away with Neosporin.

I stole school clothes and left them at Mama's house so my siblings wouldn't walk into homeroom smelling like shame. This was nothing new. Before my aunt got custody of us and I was left at home with them, I took food from the grocery store to feed us—boxed cereal, cans of ravioli—anything I could slip into a backpack without being noticed. I knew how to hide love inside the folds of stolen necessities. I knew how to survive.

My best friend and I decided we would drop out of school together. I'm not sure what we were thinking. It didn't take us long before we realized how insane this idea was.

Then at sixteen, I got pregnant.

Pregnancy didn't pause the chaos. It sharpened it. I enrolled back into school. I was so behind that it seemed impossible to catch up, but I did it. My best friend along with me. We went to regular school in the daytime, we attended night school, and we registered for alternative school. I dedicated my time to my work at school because I knew I would be having a daughter.

I eventually moved back with Mama and Daddy, not because I wanted to but because options were limited. The house reeked of stale smoke and broken promises. I watched my belly grow between thoughts of how to move out on my own, determined that my daughter would never have to live like this.

At seventeen, after she was born, I made another move. I got a job at a restaurant—pancakes and cheesy eggs—and when I filled out the application for housing, I lied. Said I was eighteen. Said I was ready. I had a baby. No one questioned it. And somehow, I got approved.

I moved into that apartment with my daughter's father. It wasn't paradise, but it was ours. He kept her while I worked overnight shifts. I'd walk in around 3 a.m. and collapse into motherhood again.

But one night, I came home and saw two black garbage bags on my doorstep. My little brother and sister stood beside them, silent except with a familiar look on their faces. Their clothes didn't match. Their eyes looked tired. They had run away from Mama and Daddy. Said they couldn't take the drug use of my parents, the noise that came with them arguing all the time, and the fear of something happening to them.

I felt so bad for them, for us. Watching them with those bags—that moment carved itself into me.

I took them in. No thought. No permission slip. No plan. Just love.

That apartment became what it was meant for—a safe space and home. I cooked what I could. Paid bills late sometimes. I worked night shifts and came home early in the mornings, cleaned, and folded our laundry while my daughter napped. I took care of all of us while barely exiting childhood. I couldn't tell at the time because it was so natural. It felt normal. But I was just a growing child myself.

What I didn't see then, but I see now, is how much of myself I gave away without even realizing it. I was growing into motherhood and sisterhood at the exact same time, trying to balance roles that should've belonged to different seasons of life. The innocence of being fourteen, fifteen, sixteen years old—it had already been traded in for responsibility.

I lived in a constant split between exhaustion and determination. At night, I was a worker; in the morning, I was a mama; and in between, I was a sister trying to hold my family together. I never stopped to think about what I needed because survival didn't leave room for that. Everything went into making sure the kids ate, the lights stayed on, and there was still love in the house no matter how messy or late the bills got.

It wasn't glamorous. It was heavy. And yet, I carried it like breathing. I thought that's what I was supposed to do. I thought it was normal to give up sleep, to make sure others had more on their plates even if mine was empty. I thought it was normal to grow up without ever getting to feel like I deserved to experience those respective stages of child development.

Later in life, I found out there was a word for this—parentification. That's when children take on adult roles far too young, becoming caretakers before they've even figured out who they are. For me, it wasn't an abstract idea in a book. It was my reality. I was doing homework with one hand while rocking a baby with the other. I was feeding my siblings before I thought about feeding myself.

Psychologists say this kind of role reversal shape's identity (Erikson, 1963, p. 25). And I can see that now. Teenagers are supposed to be discovering themselves—asking questions like, Who am I? What do I want to do with my life? I didn't have time for those questions. Mine were, how do I feed them? How do I keep us safe? My identity was built around responsibility, not self-discovery.

What's complicated is that parentification can bring both strength and scars. On one hand, it gave me resilience, empathy, and the ability to show up for people in ways many adults struggle to. On the other, it reshaped my youth into something different—not carefree or typical, but full of responsibility and love I was proud to carry. It left gaps—gaps in trust, gaps in self-care, gaps in knowing who I was when I wasn't carrying everyone else.

This is what it looks like when the door isn't locked. Kids like me step through too early, into roles that were never meant for us. It's about being reshaped by responsibilities that belonged to adults. Theory helps name it, but lived experience is what gives it weight. I wasn't extraordinary. I wasn't a hero. I was just a child raising a child, holding a family together the only way I knew how.

Theory in Practice: Redefining Adulthood Under Duress

Maslow's Hierarchy—Belonging and Responsibility:

I bypassed the usual teenage search for identity and leapt straight into roles built on care (Maslow, 1943). I wasn't just seeking belonging—I was building it. Making it from scratch, without blueprints.

Erikson's Identity vs. Role Confusion:

Adulthood didn't greet me with milestones. It greeted me with garbage bags and siblings who needed protection. My identity solidified not through self-exploration but through service (Erikson, 1963). I learned who I was by taking care of them.

Attachment Theory (Reversed):

Children typically seek attachment from caregivers. I was the child, yet my siblings attached to me (Bowlby, 1982; Bretherton, 1992). I became their safe haven. Their return to me wasn't rebellion—it was recognition. They knew where love lived.

Lessons From 3 A.M. Doorway

Sometimes the most sacred vows are made without ceremony. I didn't swear to protect them with words—I did it with meals, mattresses, and midnight talks. We trusted each other and togetherness for us was second nature and still is today. And no matter how exhausted I was, I never locked that door.

Because I knew what it felt like to arrive somewhere broken and need someone to say, "Come in."

Discussion Questions

1. What does it mean to "parent" when you're still a child yourself?
2. How does early caregiving shape identity development in adolescence?
3. Why might a lie (like saying you're eighteen) be the most honest move for survival?
4. What systems failed in allowing children to flee their home without consequence?
5. Reflect on a moment when protection demanded sacrifice. What did you gain—and what did you lose?

Comparative Overview of Human Development and Attachment Theories

Figure 1.1

Sigmund Freud's Psychosexual Stages of Development

Stage	Age Range	Erogenous Zone	Developmental Descriptions
Oral	Birth – 1 year	Mouth	Sucking, biting
Anal	1 – 3 years	Anus	Toilet training
Phallic	3 – 6 years	Genital	Identity with same-sex parent
Latency	6 – 12 years	Dormant	Socialization
Genitals	12+ years	Genitals	Intimacy, reflection

Figure 1.2

Lawrence Kohlberg's Stages of Moral Development

Levels	Age Range	Stage
Pre-conventional	3 – 7 years	Obedience and Punishment
Conventional	8 – 13 years	Social Approval and Law & Order
Post-conventional	13+ years	Social Contract and Universal Ethics

Figure 1.3

Jean Piaget's Cognitive Development of Moral Development

Stage	Age Range	Developmental Descriptions
Sensorimotor	Birth–2 years	Senses and Motor Coordination
Preoperational	2–7 years	Symbolic Thinking
Concrete Operational	7–11 years	Logic with Concrete Objects
Formal Operational	11+ years	Abstract Reason

Figure 1.4

Erik Erikson Psychosocial Stages of Development

Stage	Age Range	Developmental Descriptions
Infancy	Birth–1 year	Trust vs. Mistrust
Early Childhood	1–3 years	Autonomy vs. Shame/Doubt
Preschool	3–6 years	Initiative vs. Guilt
School Age	6–12 years	Industry vs. Inferiority
Adolescent	12–18 years	Identity vs. Role Confusion
Young Adulthood	18–40 years	Intimacy vs. Isolation
Middle Adulthood	40–65 years	Generativity vs. Stagnation
Maturity	65+ years	Ego Integrity vs. Despair

Comparative Overview of Human Development and Attachment Theories

Figure 2.1
Abraham Maslow's Hierarchy of Needs

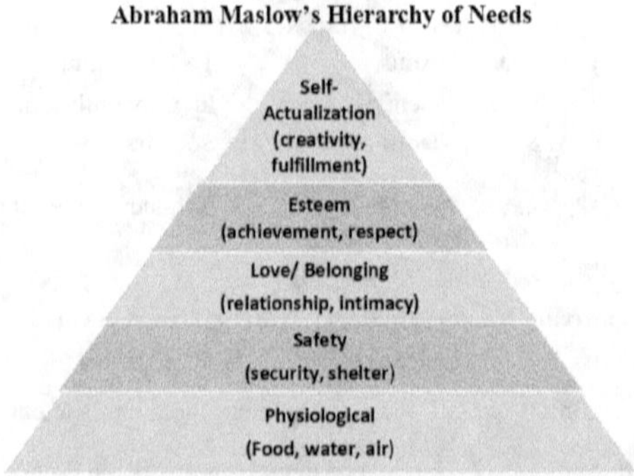

Figure 2.2
John Bowlby's Four Phases of Attachment

Phase	Age Range	Description
Pre-attachment	Birth-6 weeks	Infants show no specific attachment; respond to anyone.
Attachment-in-the-making	6 weeks - 6/8 months	Infants begin to prefer familiar caregivers; build trust.
Clear-cut attachment	6/8 months – 18/24 months	Strong attachment forms: separation anxiety and protest emerge.
Formation of reciprocal relationships	18/24 months +	Child understands caregiver's comings/goings; communication improves.

Figure 2.3
Mary Ainsworth's Attachment Syles (Strange Situation)

Attachment Styles	Behavior During Separation & Reunion
Secure	Distressed when caregiver leaves; easily comforted upon return.
Insecure-Avoidant	Shows little distress; avoids caregiver upon return.
Insecure-Resistant (ambivalent)	Very distressed; seeks contact but resists comfort. Clingy and hard to soothe.
Disorganized	Confused, fearful, or contradictory behavior. Often linked to trauma or neglect.

CHAPTER 11

Diploma in One Arm, Destiny in the Other

Theme: Victory doesn't always look polished. Sometimes it's a tired girl in a graduation gown, holding her own miracle.

I didn't walk on that stage alone. My daughter was tucked in the crook of my arm—not as baggage, not as burden but as the living proof of why I kept going. She was my reason when reason didn't make sense. The audience may have seen a teenage girl with a baby and a tassel. But that tassel was soaked in every sleepless night, every shift I worked through exhaustion, every test I took in borrowed time.

Walking across the stage, I waited for my family to get there and didn't see any of them in the crowd, but as soon as my name was called, I heard the loudest cheer from the audience. It was my family showing up for me. I'm sure they planned it this way. We like to do things like this, to put an extra umph on the surprises we give to one another. We would show up at a family's house and surprise them with another family member who came from out of town or not tell them we were coming, so they are extra surprised about the arrival. This was a normal thing for us just so we could get that big reaction. Although I was surprised to hear and see them after my name was called, I knew it was one of our signature acts of support that we have for one another. This made me feel so supported and grateful to have a family like mine. I was most honored that my mom was able to watch me walk across the stage.

Wearing that cap and gown, I felt both exhausted and alive. My robe was wrinkled, my shoes weren't new, and my arms were full, but it didn't matter. It wasn't polished, but it was proof. Every late night on the bus, every time I balanced a bottle and a book, every shift I worked when my body begged me to rest—it all landed in that moment. I wasn't supposed to be there, but I was.

People looked at me differently when they saw me holding a diploma and a baby at the same time. Some pitied me, some judged me, and a few clapped like they truly understood. But what I carried across that stage wasn't just a child and a certificate. It was evidence that the labels they put on me—"teen mom," "at risk," "high dropout probability"—didn't get the final say.

At home, life didn't slow down. The diploma didn't pay rent. The diploma didn't keep the lights on. But what it gave me was something bigger: a vision that I could build a future, even if the pieces didn't look like everyone else's. It was proof to myself that I could do hard things and finish them. And that mattered more than the paper itself.

There were no shortcuts. No saviors. Just me—working through night school, catching buses that never came on time, pushing past systems that assumed I would fail. They thought I'd become a statistic. I didn't. I became the exception that refuses to be exceptionalized. Not because I was lucky. But because I was determined.

I held my diploma close, not because it validated me—but because it proved I had authored my own ending to a chapter they tried to write for me. I didn't just graduate—I reclaimed my name from files labeled "at risk." And I did it with my child in my arms, her future braided into mine.

I didn't attend prom until the year after graduation. Although my father was still in his addiction, he went out of his way to buy me a prom dress. He also bought my daughter's father a tuxedo. This was a pretty penny to him. "Keep them tags on that dress and the tux, so I can bring them back tomorrow to get my money back", he said. I didn't care; I was just happy to even get a new dress to go to prom. I was happy that he did that for me.

Prom the following year was its own kind of milestone. I didn't step into that dress as a carefree teenager, but as a young mother who had already faced more than most people my age. My dad's gesture, even with the strings attached, showed me that love doesn't always come in the way you want it—but sometimes it's still enough. Walking into prom, I carried pride more than sparkle. I wasn't just showing up for a dance—I was showing up for the version of me that once thought I wouldn't make it that far.

Later, when I studied development theory, I realized that this moment represented something bigger. Adolescents are supposed to be going through stages of exploration, trying on different roles, and imagining different futures. For me, that stage was compressed and weighted with responsibility. I wasn't exploring who I could be—I was proving who I had to be. And yet, that diploma became a marker that even in the middle of disrupted development, growth was possible.

Graduation wasn't just a ceremony—it was a lived example of resilience. It showed how identity can be built through responsibility, how determination can override statistics, and how even early parenthood doesn't have to cancel a future. Theory might call it persistence or resilience in the face of adversity. I call it walking across a stage with a baby in my arms, claiming space in a world that once told me I had none.

Theory in Practice: Development Beyond the Expected

Maslow's Hierarchy—The Climb Isn't Linear:

The stage represents progress toward esteem and self-actualization (Maslow, 1943). But I was still climbing from the bottom—balancing safety, belonging, and dignity with each step. That diploma became a step on the ladder Maslow built—proof that even those fighting for their basic needs can still strive for fulfillment.

Erikson's Identity vs. Role Confusion:

Most adolescents are experimenting with identity. I didn't have the luxury of exploration—I had roles carved out by necessity (Erikson, 1963). But graduation gave me space to pause and claim I am more than a survivor of circumstances. I am a high school graduate. I am somebody.

Freud's Genital Stage—Rewriting Relationships:

Freud believed adolescence marked readiness for intimate relationships based on equality (Freud, 1961). But I learned that intimacy must first be safe. That love must first be chosen. My daughter taught me reciprocity before any romantic bond could.

Piaget's Formal Operational Stage:

Abstract Thinking Rooted in Reality. While others planned college majors or out-of-state new beginnings, I calculated daycare hours and budgeted grocery lists (Piaget, 1952; Huitt & Hummel, 2003). My abstract thinking was honed—not through hypothetical experiments but by surviving what was real. Graduation allowed me to finally envision something beyond crisis: curriculum, college, creation.

Lesson: The Day I Refused to Be Reduced

Graduation wasn't the finish line—it was the flag I planted in the soil of survival. A moment where dignity dressed up in a cap and gown and said, you don't get to label me. I didn't just beat odds—I bent them into a new blueprint. That diploma didn't give me power. It confirmed I already had it.

Discussion Questions

1. How does achieving educational milestones impact self-esteem in the context of Maslow's hierarchy?
2. How might Erikson's theory explain identity formation in youth caregivers and teen parents?
3. What complexities arise in intimate relationships for young survivors navigating Freud's developmental stage?
4. How can Piaget's theory be applied when abstract thinking is shaped by real-world survival rather than hypothetical reasoning?

5. Consider how cultural or systemic assumptions may distort the perception of teen mothers. What frameworks help us challenge these narratives?

Comparative Overview of Human Development and Attachment Theories

Figure 1.1

Sigmund Freud's Psychosexual Stages of Development

Stage	Age Range	Erogenous Zone	Developmental Descriptions
Oral	Birth – 1 year	Mouth	Sucking, biting
Anal	1 – 3 years	Anus	Toilet training
Phallic	3 – 6 years	Genital	Identity with same-sex parent
Latency	6 – 12 years	Dormant	Socialization
Genitals	12+ years	Genitals	Intimacy, reflection

Figure 1.2

Lawrence Kohlberg's Stages of Moral Development

Levels	Age Range	Stage
Pre-conventional	3 – 7 years	Obedience and Punishment
Conventional	8 – 13 years	Social Approval and Law & Order
Post-conventional	13+ years	Social Contract and Universal Ethics

Figure 1.3

Jean Piaget's Cognitive Development of Moral Development

Stage	Age Range	Developmental Descriptions
Sensorimotor	Birth–2 years	Senses and Motor Coordination
Preoperational	2–7 years	Symbolic Thinking
Concrete Operational	7–11 years	Logic with Concrete Objects
Formal Operational	11+ years	Abstract Reason

Figure 1.4

Erik Erikson Psychosocial Stages of Development

Stage	Age Range	Developmental Descriptions
Infancy	Birth–1 year	Trust vs. Mistrust
Early Childhood	1–3 years	Autonomy vs. Shame/Doubt
Preschool	3–6 years	Initiative vs. Guilt
School Age	6–12 years	Industry vs. Inferiority
Adolescent	12–18 years	Identity vs. Role Confusion
Young Adulthood	18–40 years	Intimacy vs. Isolation
Middle Adulthood	40–65 years	Generativity vs. Stagnation
Maturity	65+ years	Ego Integrity vs. Despair

Comparative Overview of Human Development and Attachment Theories

Figure 2.1
Abraham Maslow's Hierarchy of Needs

Figure 2.2
John Bowlby's Four Phases of Attachment

Phase	Age Range	Description
Pre-attachment	Birth-6 weeks	Infants show no specific attachment; respond to anyone.
Attachment-in-the-making	6 weeks - 6/8 months	Infants begin to prefer familiar caregivers; build trust.
Clear-cut attachment	6/8 months – 18/24 months	Strong attachment forms: separation anxiety and protest emerge.
Formation of reciprocal relationships	18/24 months +	Child understands caregiver's comings/goings; communication improves.

Figure 2.3
Mary Ainsworth's Attachment Syles (Strange Situation)

Attachment Styles	Behavior During Separation & Reunion
Secure	Distressed when caregiver leaves; easily comforted upon return.
Insecure-Avoidant	Shows little distress; avoids caregiver upon return.
Insecure-Resistant (ambivalent)	Very distressed; seeks contact but resists comfort. Clingy and hard to soothe.
Disorganized	Confused, fearful, or contradictory behavior. Often linked to trauma or neglect.

CHAPTER 12

Her Closet Wasn't Empty

Theme: Breaking cycles sometimes means bending rules—especially when love demands more than your paycheck can provide.

I left him because his breath reminded me of theirs.

My daughter's father had become a mirror of the thing I swore I'd never recreate. His drinking turned from casual to chaotic—from slurred jokes to slammed doors. I'd hear him rage, stumble, shut down. And each time, I felt my childhood tap me on the shoulder like a warning. He was becoming the environment I had fled.

So, I left.

My daughter was two. I packed us up and moved into an apartment with more willpower than square footage. There wasn't much in it—some used furniture, a mattress on the floor—but it was ours. The walls held our quiet, not someone else's noise. And in that silence, I started building something better.

It was winter when I moved into that apartment. A new year, a new start. Rent was $425, welfare gave me $437, and food stamps about $300. Just enough to pay the landlord and eat but not enough for the lights. I stretched every dollar until it hurt. I learned how to make ramen and rice feel like a full meal. I learned how to sit in the dark and pretend it was just "mood lighting." That place didn't have much, but it was mine. Nobody yelling, nobody stumbling in drunk. Just me and my daughter in the quiet.

Most days, I caught the bus, either with her bundled up on my lap or by dropping her at my mom's place so I could look for work. It wasn't what I wanted—her being there—but sometimes survival means choosing between two hard things. My mom, even throughout her addiction, found ways to help. She'd slip me a few dollars, watch my baby, do what she could. And then I'd watch her drink and feel that old anger burn. I loved her. I hated her drinking. Both these feelings lived in me at the same time.

My daughter sucked her thumb just like I did as a kid. Even in her ultrasound, her little hand was up by her mouth. Watching her do it now, I wondered if she could already feel what I carried. It was as if trauma was stitched into us before we had a choice. That thought made me push harder. I didn't want her to ever smell like poverty or walk into a room with lack written all over her.

My aunt Jean, the one who defended me along with my mom when that predator got to me and then turned right around and yelled at me when I was praying to God—yup, that one. She had stopped using drugs; her kids were returned to her; and she was in a way better space then where she was years ago when that happened to me. She started looking out for me, motivating me, giving me money, and took me to get my driver's license. At one point I lived with her. This happened between the time I left my mom's and went to live with my best friend. It was at the end of my 9th grade year. We grew a bond I didn't know was possible. By the time I got my own apartment, she acknowledged how hard I was working. She even furnished my whole house for me.

My younger siblings were older now, scattered across family placements, but still they tied me into their rhythm. They spent some weeks at my apartment, and on other weeks, we stayed in contact. We shared everything together—from groceries to clothes, along with memories stitched together from childhood stories we retold with humor to soften the blows.

I still struggled with my baby girl.

Bills didn't care that I loved her. Diapers didn't offer discounts for determination. Clothes didn't magically appear. So, I did what I had to—I stole. From stores where the security guards didn't watch me closely. Took jeans, shirts, and baby shoes. I didn't do it for fashion. I did it so my child would have what I couldn't, and to make me feel like I was doing my job as a parent. Making sure she had what she needed and what she wanted, so she wouldn't smell like poverty or walk into rooms wearing shame stitched into her sleeves.

I was crafting a reality that covered the emotional drafts I remembered.

Then, at twenty, I was arrested.

I lied to a police officer—something stupid, something small but enough to earn handcuffs. I didn't lie for fun. I lied because I didn't have a driver's license, so I used one of my cousins' names who did. I was afraid. I didn't trust officers. I grew up watching raids, hiding from sirens. My mind was wired to flinch, not cooperate.

I often felt like every step forward came with twice as many steps back. In trying to carry the weight of it all, I made choices that only masked the pain instead of healing it. Even pills couldn't ease those kinds of struggles. Everything changed after I caused a serious car accident while racing on the highway—an event that forced me to face the consequences and start taking life more seriously. It happened right after I got into a new relationship—something casual, unattached. His name—Shawn. I didn't know if I wanted commitment at that time and he certainly didn't. Even though sometimes we thought we did. We were two people experiencing something undefined, and in a way, that made sense to both of us. Commitment wasn't safe to me—it felt like a setup, a repeat of what I'd already left. So, I did what was safe for me, I let commitment define itself.

Theory in Practice: Protecting Through Resistance

Maslow's Hierarchy—Safety Meets Sacrifice:

I was trying to climb the pyramid from the bottom, holding my daughter on my hip (Maslow, 1943). Safety wasn't just about shelter—it was emotional security, dignity, and autonomy. Stealing, leaving, resisting—at that time, they weren't criminal acts to me. They were protective instincts shaped by unmet needs.

Erikson's Young Adulthood—Intimacy vs. Isolation:

At this stage, most young adults explore connections and build partnerships (Erikson, 1963). But for me, isolation was safer. Intimacy—especially after exposure to addiction and manipulation—felt risky. I guarded my heart the way I used to guard my siblings.

Erikson's describes Intimacy vs. Isolation as the central task of young adulthood (ages 18–40).

In this stage, individuals work toward deeper commitments and responsibility. Yet, unresolved struggles from the prior stage, Identity vs. Role Confusion, often bleed into this one (Erikson, 1963, p. 27).

According to Erikson's psychosocial theory, the stage of Identity vs. Role Confusion (adolescence) is marked by risk-taking behaviors and experimentation, often as a way of coping with uncertainty about self and future direction. My reliance on pills and dangerous driving reflected that struggle to manage identity and responsibility (Erikson, 1963, p. 25).

Freud's Genital Stage—Relationship Readiness and Repetition:

Freud's theory suggests that past trauma can echo in romantic patterns (Freud, 1961). I left my daughter's father because he mirrored my childhood. I hesitated with the next man because I didn't trust the patterns. I wasn't avoiding love—I was trying to redesign it.

Piaget's Formal Operational Stage—Cognitive Adaptation:

I had long mastered survival logic. My decisions were calculated—not reckless. Lying to an officer wasn't impulsive—it was a trauma-informed reaction. My brain had learned to protect first, explain later (Piaget, 1952; Huitt & Hummel, 2003).

Lessons From a Mother in Motion

I didn't get arrested because I was dangerous. I got arrested because I was scared. At this time in my life, I told myself that I didn't steal because I was careless. I stole because poverty makes thieves out of mothers who refuse to let their children feel "less."

Every choice in that chapter was stitched from a thread of love—imperfect but pure. I knew the rules. I just knew my daughter's emotional safety mattered more than those rules.

Discussion Questions

1. How do Maslow's unmet needs drive behavior often labeled as criminal?
2. What are the risks and consequences of parenting while still healing from trauma?
3. How does Erikson's theory help explain reluctance toward romantic commitment after emotional betrayal?
4. In what ways can Piaget's cognitive development model inform our understanding of trauma responses?
5. How does Erikson's idea of unfinished developmental work "bleeding" from one stage into the next help us understand why young adults may continue risky or self-destructive behaviors even after adolescence?

Comparative Overview of Human Development and Attachment Theories

Figure 1.1

Sigmund Freud's Psychosexual Stages of Development

Stage	Age Range	Erogenous Zone	Developmental Descriptions
Oral	Birth – 1 year	Mouth	Sucking, biting
Anal	1 – 3 years	Anus	Toilet training
Phallic	3 – 6 years	Genital	Identity with same-sex parent
Latency	6 – 12 years	Dormant	Socialization
Genitals	12+ years	Genitals	Intimacy, reflection

Figure 1.2

Lawrence Kohlberg's Stages of Moral Development

Levels	Age Range	Stage
Pre-conventional	3 – 7 years	Obedience and Punishment
Conventional	8 – 13 years	Social Approval and Law & Order
Post-conventional	13+ years	Social Contract and Universal Ethics

Figure 1.3

Jean Piaget's Cognitive Development of Moral Development

Stage	Age Range	Developmental Descriptions
Sensorimotor	Birth–2 years	Senses and Motor Coordination
Preoperational	2–7 years	Symbolic Thinking
Concrete Operational	7–11 years	Logic with Concrete Objects
Formal Operational	11+ years	Abstract Reason

Figure 1.4

Erik Erikson Psychosocial Stages of Development

Stage	Age Range	Developmental Descriptions
Infancy	Birth–1 year	Trust vs. Mistrust
Early Childhood	1–3 years	Autonomy vs. Shame/Doubt
Preschool	3–6 years	Initiative vs. Guilt
School Age	6–12 years	Industry vs. Inferiority
Adolescent	12–18 years	Identity vs. Role Confusion
Young Adulthood	18–40 years	Intimacy vs. Isolation
Middle Adulthood	40–65 years	Generativity vs. Stagnation
Maturity	65+ years	Ego Integrity vs. Despair

Comparative Overview of Human Development and Attachment Theories

Figure 2.1
Abraham Maslow's Hierarchy of Needs

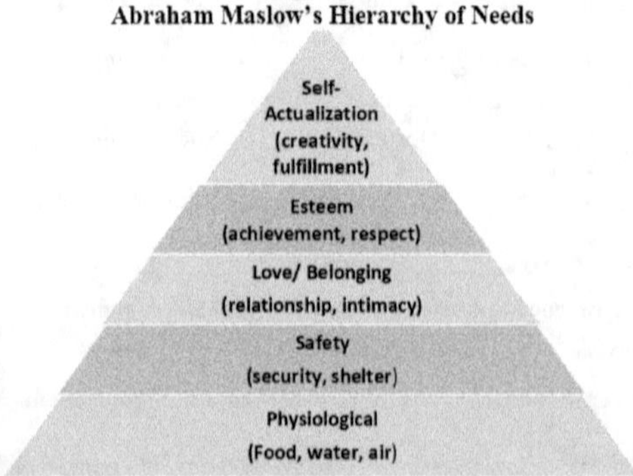

Figure 2.2
John Bowlby's Four Phases of Attachment

Phase	Age Range	Description
Pre-attachment	Birth-6 weeks	Infants show no specific attachment; respond to anyone.
Attachment-in-the-making	6 weeks - 6/8 months	Infants begin to prefer familiar caregivers; build trust.
Clear-cut attachment	6/8 months – 18/24 months	Strong attachment forms: separation anxiety and protest emerge.
Formation of reciprocal relationships	18/24 months +	Child understands caregiver's comings/goings; communication improves.

Figure 2.3
Mary Ainsworth's Attachment Syles (Strange Situation)

Attachment Styles	Behavior During Separation & Reunion
Secure	Distressed when caregiver leaves; easily comforted upon return.
Insecure-Avoidant	Shows little distress; avoids caregiver upon return.
Insecure-Resistant (ambivalent)	Very distressed; seeks contact but resists comfort. Clingy and hard to soothe.
Disorganized	Confused, fearful, or contradictory behavior. Often linked to trauma or neglect.

CHAPTER 13

The Christmas That Cost Me Everything

Theme: When devotion drives defiance, and motherhood becomes both motive and measure of redemption.

I was supposed to keep my record spotless, clear, and be careful of who I was around—for a year. But my relationship with Shawn felt like a new kind of safety. He didn't drink. That alone felt like hitting the jackpot. I didn't have to brace myself for shouting matches or blackout blame.

We smoked weed, sure. But for me it was mild. Quiet. Familiar.

He came with pain but it matched mine—not dismissed mine. We didn't push each other to be better; we held space until better felt possible. And then—life expanded. A baby boy. A home. A deeper kind of partnership.

He showed up whenever I needed him to.

Through fights. Through strained finances. Through shame. We stayed together. Even when I tried to push him away, he stayed. And even though I didn't realize it at the time, staying meant something to me. It meant everything.

We did what we had to do. He sold drugs. I wrote checks that weren't mine. Not for handbags or getaways—for diapers, for food, for Christmas magic. For joy in a living room we had furnished with effort, not elegance.

I was arrested again—for a check that I wrote when I knew my account was closed. I wrote this check with love disguised as desperation. My daughter was seven. My son was two. I wanted them to wake up to gifts under a tree so dazzling it erased every doubt they might've had about where they came from.

I went back on probation. Five years, this time—probation became another kind of hustle. I showed up to my officer once a month at first, checking boxes, saying the right words, nodding at the right time. After a while, I earned the right to check in by phone, which felt like freedom I hadn't really earned. I knew how to sound like a stand-up citizen even when my life was anything but upstanding. Survival doesn't always show up on paperwork.

Then he moved out of town, and I moved with him—not chasing a man but chasing consistency. He was making money. And even though the money came fast and dirty, it made things feel stable, momentarily.

I thought back to when my dad first showed me how to make money. This was before I had my daughter. He had me give him the money so he could get the drugs to give to some of his friends, and he would give me more money back than I gave him. He was showing me how fast cash moved in the streets. At first it looked easy—money in, money out—but it never stayed clean. I'd get shorted, cheated, reminded real quick that loyalty didn't exist when addiction was in the mix. Watching my dad take his cut, watching him use, showed me the ugly side of hustling. That's when I told myself, I wanted no part of it. But the lesson stuck in me anyway. Poverty will push you back toward things you swore you'd never touch, and sometimes survival sounds just like the voices you tried to escape.

After a year of being in this new town, we had another baby boy. Now I was a mother of three, and I was worried about our lifestyle. I told Shawn I couldn't stay in the apartment anymore and although he planned to give it all up, it wasn't happening quickly enough for me. I told him I was going into a shelter until I could find another place for us to be in a safer environment.

It felt good, until it wasn't. It finally happened. The police kicked our door down.

The raid shattered the illusion. They found it all. They found everything he was selling, everything that paid for the furniture—those shoes, that closet full of clothes. And just like that, jail—rock bottom wasn't a metaphor. It was my new mailing address.

Even now, my body remembers the way it went numb when I realized the police were inside. By that time, I had already taken my kids into a shelter because I felt the walls closing in at the old house. I knew what Shawn was doing, and I knew it wasn't safe. He promised me he was slowing down, promised he'd clear it all out. I wanted to believe him. I wanted stability, not chaos.

The day it happened; we had just gone to get food. The kids were still at the apartment when the police pulled us over. My stomach dropped when they said they were inside the home. All I could think was—my babies were in there. I didn't know at the time that my sister, who lived next door, had already gone in to get them out. For those first few hours, I was trapped in the worst fear a mother could have.

They didn't care that I was living in the shelter. They didn't care that I said I was just visiting. They knew I knew what was happening, so I was taken in right along with Shawn. Jail became my new mailing address.

And still, God didn't disappear. Locked up, I turned to the only thing that steadied me: His Word. I read the entire Bible, cover to cover. I remember one night waking up in my cell and hearing one word as loud as if someone had shouted it: ACCEPTANCE. I wrestled with it—angry, ashamed, replaying every choice that put my kids and me in that mess. But that word stayed. I had to accept the nightmare in order to move through it. Acceptance didn't mean I agreed with it. It meant I stopped fighting the reality of where I was so I could start fighting for where I needed to be.

Cycles don't just repeat—they test every line between survival and surrender. Theory gives language to that tension, but I lived it first in probation offices, Christmas mornings, and jail cells.

Theory in Practice: Rock Bottom as Rebirth

Maslow's Hierarchy—Love Over Law:

Sometimes love drives behavior that defies rules (Maslow, 1943). I wasn't trying to bypass the system—I was trying to build one of my own. One where needs were met and Christmas came with dignity. This chapter is where Maslow's pyramid meets the reality of being poor and protective.

Erikson's Generativity vs. Stagnation:

Though young adulthood usually explores intimacy, motherhood shifted me straight into generativity (Erikson, 1963). I was nurturing others—but the struggle to avoid stagnation meant playing roles I never wanted: hustler, survivor, defendant.

Freud—Defense Mechanisms and Emotional Logic:

My denial of risk wasn't naivety—it was a defense. I rationalized criminal acts through a lens of love and caregiving. The mind finds ways to protect itself when your intentions are noble, but your means are not (Freud, 1961).

Piaget—Post-Traumatic Decision-Making:

My cognition had adapted to crisis. The logic of those decisions may not align with societal norms, but they were built from emotional truths: children need, and mothers respond (Piaget, 1952; Huitt & Hummel, 2003).

Lessons From the Lowest Point

Rock bottom isn't quiet.

It's loud with regrets. Heavy with flashbacks. Cold with fear. But it also has clarity. Because when the distractions are gone, and the chaos gets arrested, you have to face what's left.

And what was left for me?

Three kids. A love that tried. A sister who showed up. And a future that hadn't left yet.

Discussion Questions

1. How do society's rules conflict with parental instinct in high-pressure situations?

2. Can survival-driven crime be reframed as protective caregiving in developmental terms?
3. What role does generational trauma play in shaping definitions of commitment and trust?
4. How do Freud's and Piaget's theories help explain high-risk decision-making under emotional duress?
5. How might "rock bottom" mark the start of authentic self-awareness and transformation?

Comparative Overview of Human Development and Attachment Theories

Figure 1.1

Sigmund Freud's Psychosexual Stages of Development

Stage	Age Range	Erogenous Zone	Developmental Descriptions
Oral	Birth – 1 year	Mouth	Sucking, biting
Anal	1 – 3 years	Anus	Toilet training
Phallic	3 – 6 years	Genital	Identity with same-sex parent
Latency	6 – 12 years	Dormant	Socialization
Genitals	12+ years	Genitals	Intimacy, reflection

Figure 1.2

Lawrence Kohlberg's Stages of Moral Development

Levels	Age Range	Stage
Pre-conventional	3 – 7 years	Obedience and Punishment
Conventional	8 – 13 years	Social Approval and Law & Order
Post-conventional	13+ years	Social Contract and Universal Ethics

Figure 1.3

Jean Piaget's Cognitive Development of Moral Development

Stage	Age Range	Developmental Descriptions
Sensorimotor	Birth–2 years	Senses and Motor Coordination
Preoperational	2–7 years	Symbolic Thinking
Concrete Operational	7–11 years	Logic with Concrete Objects
Formal Operational	11+ years	Abstract Reason

Figure 1.4

Erik Erikson Psychosocial Stages of Development

Stage	Age Range	Developmental Descriptions
Infancy	Birth–1 year	Trust vs. Mistrust
Early Childhood	1–3 years	Autonomy vs. Shame/Doubt
Preschool	3–6 years	Initiative vs. Guilt
School Age	6–12 years	Industry vs. Inferiority
Adolescent	12–18 years	Identity vs. Role Confusion
Young Adulthood	18–40 years	Intimacy vs. Isolation
Middle Adulthood	40–65 years	Generativity vs. Stagnation
Maturity	65+ years	Ego Integrity vs. Despair

Comparative Overview of Human Development and Attachment Theories

Figure 2.1
Abraham Maslow's Hierarchy of Needs

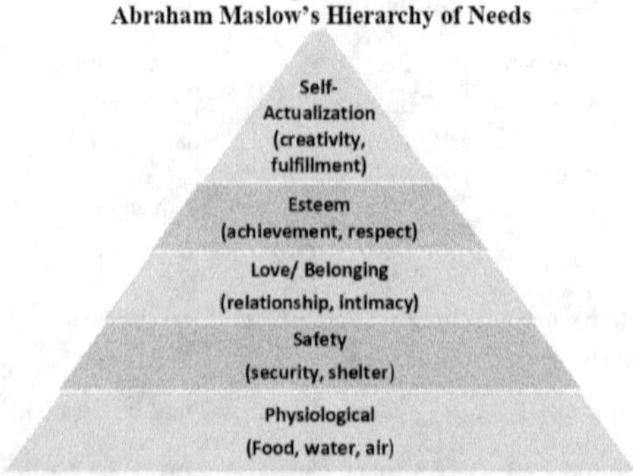

Figure 2.2
John Bowlby's Four Phases of Attachment

Phase	Age Range	Description
Pre-attachment	Birth-6 weeks	Infants show no specific attachment; respond to anyone.
Attachment-in-the-making	6 weeks - 6/8 months	Infants begin to prefer familiar caregivers; build trust.
Clear-cut attachment	6/8 months – 18/24 months	Strong attachment forms: separation anxiety and protest emerge.
Formation of reciprocal relationships	18/24 months +	Child understands caregiver's comings/goings; communication improves.

Figure 2.3
Mary Ainsworth's Attachment Syles (Strange Situation)

Attachment Styles	Behavior During Separation & Reunion
Secure	Distressed when caregiver leaves; easily comforted upon return.
Insecure-Avoidant	Shows little distress; avoids caregiver upon return.
Insecure-Resistant (ambivalent)	Very distressed; seeks contact but resists comfort. Clingy and hard to soothe.
Disorganized	Confused, fearful, or contradictory behavior. Often linked to trauma or neglect.

CHAPTER 14

Calls from a Cell and Echoes from Childhood

Theme: The darkest places sometimes cradle the first stirrings of light.

The steel bench was colder than I expected. Concrete walls didn't speak, but they listened. My body was booked, fingerprinted, processed. But my mind had already fled—to my children. Not the court date. Not the charges. Just: Where are my babies?

My sister had kept them safe through the chaos, and as soon as I heard her voice, I gave instructions like a mother in wartime. "Call my mama. Tell her everything. Tell her to get my babies." Sitting in that cell, shame wrapped itself around me tighter than the jail-issued blanket. I had always promised myself—and silently promised my children—that I would never be the kind of mother who handed down trauma like hand-me-down clothes.

And yet here I was. Arrested. Absent. Aching. And they were innocent. Sleeping somewhere without me.

As a little girl, my most consistent prayer wasn't about toys or birthdays—it was that my parents would get clean. I used to imagine it in quiet moments: a sober household, a peaceful dinner table, laughter that wasn't stretched thin by addiction. By the time I had children of my own, that dream hadn't died—it just dulled. I tucked it away behind bills and night shifts and moments of my own survival.

Then came whispers. While I was living out of town, I heard that they had moved. A couple hours outside their old stomping grounds. A quiet place. No familiar corners. No neighborhood names whispered in backroom deals. I heard they weren't using anymore. But I didn't believe it—not at first. I'd seen too much. Buried too many hopes.

"They came," my sister said. "Right away. Picked up the kids. Took them home." When I called and my mom picked up, her voice cut through me. It wasn't shaky or blurred or slowed by the substances I had grown up fearing. It was steady. It was sober.

"They're okay, baby," she said. "You don't have to worry."

Her tone didn't just lessen my panic—it cracked something open in me. A kind of possibility I hadn't felt in years. For the next six months, I called every other day. My kids sounded happy. Their voices didn't carry fear. This put me at ease.

I signed up for every class the jail offered—parenting, healing, trauma recovery—anything that felt like I was moving forward. The most impactful program for me was the trauma-focused cognitive behavioral therapy to address the sexual assault that I experienced. This helped me dramatically. It gave me my voice back. I was able to talk about it out loud. I got to a point where I could talk about it without tearing up.

On some days, I would call Daddy and get a lesson from him. My daddy spoke to me with clarity, not confusion. He told me about his own time inside prison. Not with pride—but with perspective. He told me to keep moving. Told me that rehabilitation was real. That what I was experiencing wasn't the end—it was the interruption before a new beginning.

It didn't erase what I'd done. But it stitched something back together in me.

I began to question how I got here, doing time in jail. "Why was I making these awful decisions?" This was the moment that I realized the only role model that I ever had was the adults around me doing everything that I didn't want to do. I sat in jail wondering, what if I had someone to just tell me not to steal, not to lie to a police officer, not to do things that would ruin my future. I thought to myself, what if I had someone in my life to set a good example for me, so I could avoid jail. By this time, I was a young adult and already on my second felony. Why was I just now connecting the dots. I realized I had been surviving all these years and doing the best I could with what I had—And that wasn't much.

After sitting in jail in Iowa for five long months, Shawn's father put up his home so I could make bail. While I was inside, I took classes—sexual assault awareness and behavioral therapy. For the first time, I was able to speak openly about what I had been through. Jail wasn't healing, but it gave me language for some of the weight I carried.

When I was released, I went straight back to Minnesota to pick up my children from my mom. The moment I saw them; I felt grace I didn't deserve. Their arms wrapped tight around me, faces pressed into me—it felt like touching hope again. My sister let us stay with her for a while, but soon I went back into the same shelter I had lived in before the raid.

Shelter life had its own rhythm. Getting the kids off to school early in the morning, then starting work during the day, and going back to the shelter at night. It wasn't permanent, but it was safe enough to keep me going. The staff became my lifeline. They stood by me at every hearing, showing the court that I wasn't running from accountability—I was trying to rebuild.

At sentencing in Iowa, I walked into that courtroom ready for eighteen months behind bars. I knew what I had been around, and in my head, I was already bracing for jail. But I prayed. The judge looked at me and then told me to turn around. The officer behind me was holding pink handcuffs. My heart froze. Then the judge said, "Those cuffs are meant for you—but because this advocate has stood up and spoke about your growth, because your children and sister are here in court in support of you, and because I believe in giving people a second chance I will give you a stayed sentence and probation instead."

I broke down crying, thanking him through tears. That moment didn't erase everything I had done, but it showed me what mercy could look like when somebody believed in your change.

Not long after, the police came to the shelter with a warrant—this time from Minnesota, where I had violated my probation. But the advocates refused to let them in. They protected me and, more importantly, they protected my children from another scene of flashing lights and trauma. Instead, they bought me a bus ticket and made sure I could settle my kids before turning myself in.

When I finally stood in a Minnesota courtroom, the outcome was different. This time, I was sentenced to prison. The pain wasn't for me—it was for my kids. Leaving them again felt like ripping open the same wound twice. But under the heartbreak was something else: relief. I didn't have to live waiting for the hammer to drop. No more looking over my shoulder. If prison was the road in front of me, at least it was clear.

I had violated my five-year probation—not just by catching another charge but by relocating out of state without permission. My actions had consequences, and the system didn't forget.

I had just been released from jail two months prior. The judge didn't care that I just did five months in jail, that I obtained a job, or that I voluntarily turned myself in. He was sending me to prison. This time I wasn't as numb as I was when I was in jail—but it wasn't a cake walk either.

I felt forced away from my children, yet again. I just wanted to do my time and fast forward to being home with my babies. I knew what I needed to do. I started realizing that I was put there for a reason. Like someone had finally noticed how heavy of a burden I'd been carrying around. And while prison isn't justice, and it certainly isn't healing, it became another place where I had to sit still long enough to figure out who I was without all the noise.

Behind bars again, I saw it differently. I wasn't hiding—I was being held still.

My sister, my mom's youngest daughter, kept my youngest son; my aunt who helped raise me sent my two older kids to school from her house, while my parents kept them during the summer. They held it down. My mother turned discipline into routine. My father offered advice that came from scars, not theories. And I realized: The people who once wounded me were now holding what I loved most.

That contradiction still stings. But it also gives me hope. That people can change. That time can reroute things. And that redemption doesn't have to be loud—it can speak in bedtime stories, car rides home from school, or steady phone calls.

That's what systems do—they stack on top of each other, crashing into your life in ways that hit children the hardest. I accept all accountability for what I did without offering excuses, just facts to support some of the theories I've learned about. And that season also taught me that survival isn't only about grit—it's about protection. It's about shelters, advocates, and the rare people who fight for you when you can't fight for yourself. Trauma theory calls these protective factors—the people, places, and structures that interrupt the cycle long enough for you to breathe (van der Kolk, 2003). For me, it was a shelter staff that refused to open their doors, a judge who chose mercy, and children who reminded me I still had a reason to keep going.

Theory in Practice: Reversals, Repairs, and Reparenting

Erikson's Identity vs. Role Confusion:

Jail forced reflection. Who was I? A mother? A criminal? A child still chasing old hopes? This chapter captures the tension between roles—how developmental identity fractures and reforms under crisis (Erikson, 1963).

Attachment Theory:

My bond with my children stayed strong through consistent communication and reassurance. Even amid trauma, attachment was still preserved to some extent—through routines, loving words, and family presence. It's proof that attachment repair is possible, even during separation (Bowlby, 1982; Bretherton, 1992).

Maslow's Hierarchy—Return to Safety:

In jail, I couldn't meet every need—but I could rebuild emotional safety (Maslow, 1943). That became my new center, knowing they were warm, fed, and surrounded by sober love.

Freud's Legacy—Unconscious Drive for Redemption:

My plea to my mom wasn't just practical—it was primal (Freud, 1961). A subconscious desire for generational healing. My actions were born of pain, but my instincts were reaching for repair.

Lessons From Lockdown

The bars weren't the most painful part. It was the ache of knowing I'd repeated what I swore I'd never do. But the calls from my kids—bright and loving—whispered grace. I didn't have the power to erase their fear. But I could show up, even from behind walls.

And when I stepped out, I faced a judge. Violated probation. Moved without permission. Caught new charges.

"A year and a day," the court said.

But I'd already started doing time in my spirit. Now I'd finish it with purpose.

Discussion Questions

1. How does parental sobriety change the trajectory of generational trauma?
2. In what ways can secure attachment be preserved or repaired during parental incarceration?
3. How does Erikson's theory illuminate the fluid identity of justice-involved parents?

4. What role does forgiveness—both of self and others—play in recovery and reunification?
5. Consider how trauma shapes parenting. Can intention rewrite instinct?

Comparative Overview
of Human Development and Attachment Theories

Figure 1.1

Sigmund Freud's Psychosexual Stages of Development

Stage	Age Range	Erogenous Zone	Developmental Descriptions
Oral	Birth – 1 year	Mouth	Sucking, biting
Anal	1 – 3 years	Anus	Toilet training
Phallic	3 – 6 years	Genital	Identity with same-sex parent
Latency	6 – 12 years	Dormant	Socialization
Genitals	12+ years	Genitals	Intimacy, reflection

Figure 1.2

Lawrence Kohlberg's Stages of Moral Development

Levels	Age Range	Stage
Pre-conventional	3 – 7 years	Obedience and Punishment
Conventional	8 – 13 years	Social Approval and Law & Order
Post-conventional	13+ years	Social Contract and Universal Ethics

Figure 1.3

Jean Piaget's Cognitive Development of Moral Development

Stage	Age Range	Developmental Descriptions
Sensorimotor	Birth–2 years	Senses and Motor Coordination
Preoperational	2–7 years	Symbolic Thinking
Concrete Operational	7–11 years	Logic with Concrete Objects
Formal Operational	11+ years	Abstract Reason

Figure 1.4

Erik Erikson Psychosocial Stages of Development

Stage	Age Range	Developmental Descriptions
Infancy	Birth–1 year	Trust vs. Mistrust
Early Childhood	1–3 years	Autonomy vs. Shame/Doubt
Preschool	3–6 years	Initiative vs. Guilt
School Age	6–12 years	Industry vs. Inferiority
Adolescent	12–18 years	Identity vs. Role Confusion
Young Adulthood	18–40 years	Intimacy vs. Isolation
Middle Adulthood	40–65 years	Generativity vs. Stagnation
Maturity	65+ years	Ego Integrity vs. Despair

Comparative Overview of Human Development and Attachment Theories

Figure 2.1
Abraham Maslow's Hierarchy of Needs

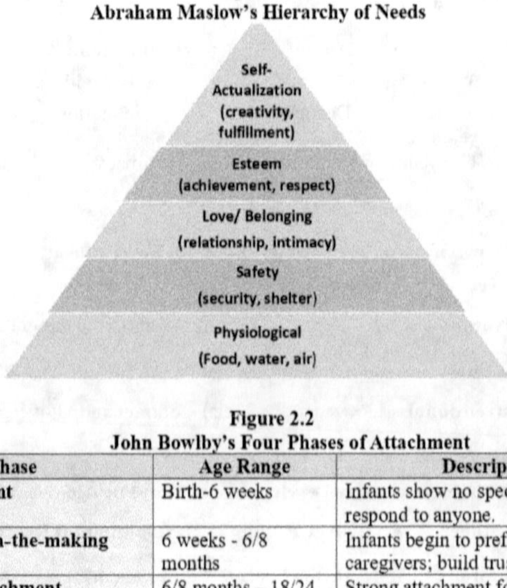

Figure 2.2
John Bowlby's Four Phases of Attachment

Phase	Age Range	Description
Pre-attachment	Birth-6 weeks	Infants show no specific attachment; respond to anyone.
Attachment-in-the-making	6 weeks - 6/8 months	Infants begin to prefer familiar caregivers; build trust.
Clear-cut attachment	6/8 months – 18/24 months	Strong attachment forms: separation anxiety and protest emerge.
Formation of reciprocal relationships	18/24 months +	Child understands caregiver's comings/goings; communication improves.

Figure 2.3
Mary Ainsworth's Attachment Syles (Strange Situation)

Attachment Styles	Behavior During Separation & Reunion
Secure	Distressed when caregiver leaves; easily comforted upon return.
Insecure-Avoidant	Shows little distress; avoids caregiver upon return.
Insecure-Resistant (ambivalent)	Very distressed; seeks contact but resists comfort. Clingy and hard to soothe.
Disorganized	Confused, fearful, or contradictory behavior. Often linked to trauma or neglect.

CHAPTER 15

The Promise of Presence

Theme: Healing begins not with grand gestures but with consistent returns.

They called it reentry. The system's word for stepping back into society after prison. But for me, it felt more like restoration. Not because everything was fixed—but because something had shifted. I had evidence. Six credits from taking two college courses while in prison. It wasn't a degree—but it was proof. Proof that I could still grow. Still learn. Still finish something.

My children's father was still locked up—doing two more years. We had made vows: to do it right this time. To stay together. To choose our family over chaos. And I did stay. But I also stepped into the work of rebuilding myself. Of cleaning up the pieces I had scattered during the storm.

The halfway house had been my first stop after release, and I'll never forget the officer pulling into a gas station on the way there. I hadn't seen a different scenery in months. The sky looked brighter, the air smelled sharper, even the sound of traffic felt alive. Freedom didn't announce itself with trumpets—it hummed in small things, like the buzz of a gas pump or the wind pushing through an open window.

The halfway house staff wasn't gentle. They were waiting for any slip to send you back. But I wasn't going back. I held my head down, did what I needed to do, and focused on moving forward. Within weeks, I got a job. My sister brought my children to visit me every week, and those visits stitched me back into their lives piece by piece.

When we were finally settled into our new apartment after prison, the older kids seemed to adjust quickly. They were practiced at weathering change. But my youngest son? He needed something different. He had been little when I left. Still sticky-fingered and wide-eyed. He had talked to me on the phone, knew my voice. But when I stood in front of him again—he hesitated. I had gained weight. My face had softened. I wasn't the mom he had memorized.

After I got out of jail and came to Minnesota to pick up my children the first time, before going to prison, my youngest son didn't remember me. My daughter showed him a picture—pointed to me. He looked up. Blinked. Stared. Then, after thirty long seconds, he jumped into my arms. His hug was tight, desperate, and longing. So when I picked him up from my sister, after getting out of prison, he clung to me like I might vanish. And I understood—because I had.

From that day forward, he shadowed me. If I walked into the bathroom, he followed. If I went to get a glass of water, he reached for my hand. He couldn't afford not to know where I was. So I started explaining my every move, because this is what he needed. "I'm getting a cup of water—I'll be right back." "I'm taking a bath—I'll be right back." And then I showed up. He was still searching for proof. And so I became proof. Proof that I could come back when I said I would. Proof that I would return after work, after class, after running an errand. Every ordinary action became a way to rebuild trust. That's how healing looked for us—quiet, steady, almost boring in its repetition. And yet, it was powerful.

His trust wasn't rebuilt by grand declarations. It was restored by consistency. By every moment I kept my word. By every bath I returned from. Every errand I ended with a hug. After about a year, something shifted. He stopped watching me so closely. Because he knew I wouldn't disappear again.

A year out of prison, I made a decision. I moved two hours outside the city. Quiet town. Slower pace. A fresh start. I didn't cut ties. I visited my mom, stayed connected to my roots. But I knew I couldn't heal in the same places that had witnessed my worst. I needed somewhere my children could thrive without the echo of my former life.

It wasn't abandonment, it was intentional. And for the first time, I moved because it was what was right for me so that I could do right for my children.

Moving two hours out of the city was my way of planting something new. I knew what I was used to, but had grew out of—the chaos, the old memories, the drama. I didn't want my kids to grow up hearing that echo. I wanted them to hear something else: peace, safety, consistency. It wasn't about running from my roots. It was about giving my children the chance to grow in soil that hadn't already been poisoned.

Attachment theory calls this repair—when broken trust is restored through consistent presence and reliability (Bowlby, 1982; Bretherton, 1992). For my son, it wasn't my words that convinced him, it was my actions. For my family, it wasn't a relocation that healed us but the intention behind it: a choice to prioritize growth over comfort, stability over familiarity. Reentry may have been the system's word, but for us it meant restoration—showing that love could return, stay, and keep showing up day after day.

Theory in Practice: Presence, Growth, and Real Attachment Work

Attachment Theory—Consistency as Care:

My youngest son's response after my release illustrates a classic insecure attachment reaction—anxiety, clinginess, fear of abandonment. But through consistent behavior and verbal reassurance, I helped him transition toward secure attachment, rebuilding his ability to trust that caregivers return (Bowlby, 1982; Bretherton, 1992). I hadn't studied any of the theories behind attachment during this time; I simply responded to what he needed. The routine we built became living evidence that the theory was right—that trust can be rebuilt through presence, consistency, and care.

Erikson's Generativity vs. Stagnation:

This stage emerged not in speeches or plans, but in quiet moments of care (Erikson, 1963). Generativity showed up in bedtime routines, stable housing, and healing interaction. I was no longer surviving—I was investing.

Lessons in Movement

Healing after incarceration is rarely linear. It's not dramatic—it's gradual. It happens in bath-taking, getting water, and hugs held too long. In staying. In repeating. In returning. It happens when a child says, "Are you coming back?" And the answer is, "Always."

Discussion Questions

1. How does consistency in behavior rebuild trust in child-parent relationships?
2. In what ways does personal achievement (like college credits) impact self-identity after incarceration?
3. How do attachment dynamics shift when a caregiver returns after absence?
4. What does "intentional distance" look like in breaking generational cycles?
5. How can Maslow's Hierarchy be used to map reentry success and emotional recovery?

Comparative Overview
of Human Development and Attachment Theories

Figure 1.1

Sigmund Freud's Psychosexual Stages of Development

Stage	Age Range	Erogenous Zone	Developmental Descriptions
Oral	Birth – 1 year	Mouth	Sucking, biting
Anal	1 – 3 years	Anus	Toilet training
Phallic	3 – 6 years	Genital	Identity with same-sex parent
Latency	6 – 12 years	Dormant	Socialization
Genitals	12+ years	Genitals	Intimacy, reflection

Figure 1.2

Lawrence Kohlberg's Stages of Moral Development

Levels	Age Range	Stage
Pre-conventional	3 – 7 years	Obedience and Punishment
Conventional	8 – 13 years	Social Approval and Law & Order
Post-conventional	13+ years	Social Contract and Universal Ethics

Figure 1.3

Jean Piaget's Cognitive Development of Moral Development

Stage	Age Range	Developmental Descriptions
Sensorimotor	Birth–2 years	Senses and Motor Coordination
Preoperational	2–7 years	Symbolic Thinking
Concrete Operational	7–11 years	Logic with Concrete Objects
Formal Operational	11+ years	Abstract Reason

Figure 1.4

Erik Erikson Psychosocial Stages of Development

Stage	Age Range	Developmental Descriptions
Infancy	Birth–1 year	Trust vs. Mistrust
Early Childhood	1–3 years	Autonomy vs. Shame/Doubt
Preschool	3–6 years	Initiative vs. Guilt
School Age	6–12 years	Industry vs. Inferiority
Adolescent	12–18 years	Identity vs. Role Confusion
Young Adulthood	18–40 years	Intimacy vs. Isolation
Middle Adulthood	40–65 years	Generativity vs. Stagnation
Maturity	65+ years	Ego Integrity vs. Despair

Comparative Overview of Human Development and Attachment Theories

Figure 2.1
Abraham Maslow's Hierarchy of Needs

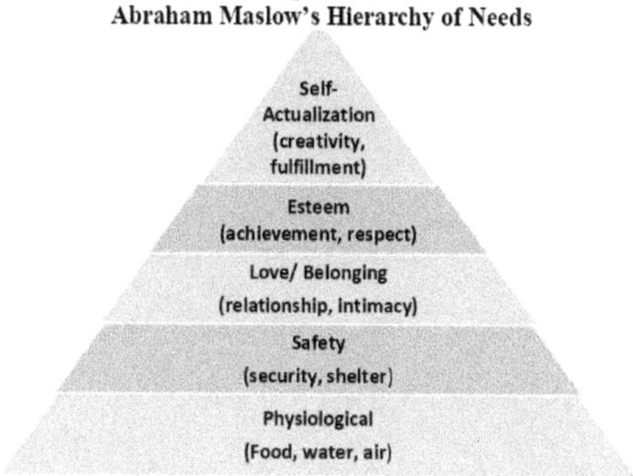

Figure 2.2
John Bowlby's Four Phases of Attachment

Phase	Age Range	Description
Pre-attachment	Birth-6 weeks	Infants show no specific attachment; respond to anyone.
Attachment-in-the-making	6 weeks - 6/8 months	Infants begin to prefer familiar caregivers; build trust.
Clear-cut attachment	6/8 months – 18/24 months	Strong attachment forms: separation anxiety and protest emerge.
Formation of reciprocal relationships	18/24 months +	Child understands caregiver's comings/goings; communication improves.

Figure 2.3
Mary Ainsworth's Attachment Syles (Strange Situation)

Attachment Styles	Behavior During Separation & Reunion
Secure	Distressed when caregiver leaves; easily comforted upon return.
Insecure-Avoidant	Shows little distress; avoids caregiver upon return.
Insecure-Resistant (ambivalent)	Very distressed; seeks contact but resists comfort. Clingy and hard to soothe.
Disorganized	Confused, fearful, or contradictory behavior. Often linked to trauma or neglect.

CHAPTER 16

Permission to Rise

Theme: Dignity doesn't come from approval—it's reclaimed by refusal.

Three years into Duluth, MN, and it finally seemed like we found solid ground. My boys' father had finished his sentence and finally joined us. We worked. We parented. We honored our vow: to do things right. For once, the chaos wasn't at our doorstep—it was quiet, folded into routine.

I decided I wanted something to show for all the forward motion. Not just resilience—but credentials. An associate's degree. Something my kids could point to and say, Mama did that. Something that said I'd fought for more than survival.

I was told that if I entered into the vocational rehabilitation program they could help with school. Prior to me finding this out, it was recommended that I reach out to my job counselor to get help with school. They had a program specifically for low-income people who received county assistance. I was excited to obtain the support that could help me get into school. But when I walked into her office, I felt the shift immediately. I was right on time for my appointment. She barely looked up. Her posture said inconvenient. Her questions came clipped—"Name?" "Age?" "Kids?" No warmth. No curiosity. Just a checklist.

I told her I wanted to enter a computer technology program. I knew what I wanted. I just needed help navigating the paperwork. Before I finished the sentence, she said, "No. We don't pay for that." I offered another option. She cut me off. "Nope. Not covered." Her unconcerned attitude toward me made me feel hopeless at this moment. I had learned to hold my tongue so that I didn't jeopardize being put back in jail and separated from my children again. I was trying to be more reserved. I asked in a frustrated voice, "What do you support then?" She slid a thick packet across the desk like it was a burden she was trying to get rid of. "Go look these over and find something we help with. Make another appointment and come back." Without making a scene, I took the packet and left.

It wasn't guidance—it was dismissal.

Before I made it home, she called me. When I answered, she explained, "There's a center" she said, "It's on the other side of town. It helps people of color. Might fit your needs better." I froze. Did she really say that out loud? At this point, I had enough of reserving my frustrations. When I confronted her, I wasn't anxious. My voice didn't shake. I was steady. Firm. I told her how she had treated me, how her words landed. She didn't apologize. Didn't even flicker. For the first time since I'd started this process, I thought about giving up.

I let her know how unprofessional she had been since I first walked through the door. I questioned why she was sending me to a different organization.

"That sounds like segregation," I said. She'd decided the moment I met with her in her office earlier that day, that I wasn't her responsibility.

I wasn't about to be rerouted without fighting first.

I marched back into her office a few days later and pointed at the human services program. "This program is listed. I would like to sign up for this one." She scanned it and shrugged her shoulders. "You won't make more than nine or ten dollars in that field. I'm not recommending it." That's when it hit me—this wasn't about funding or the program not being eligible for me to take. It was about gatekeeping. I felt like she didn't think I belonged in the human service field or any field of work. I realized her goal was to keep me right where I was. This program was fully acceptable, and she decided I shouldn't take it. She wanted my dreams to shrink. I reached out to so many people to try to file grievances, and it just seemed like it was a never-ending process.

I felt drained, but I was still walking, each step heavier than the last.

Feeling defeated, I finally found my way to the other center and met with a worker who couldn't offer any type of guidance. At this time, I was fed up and just ready to give up on trying to go to school.

I started walking toward the door in a state of exhaustion, but before I could get to the door, a lady who could hear my frustration came around the corner and asked me to sit with her in her cubical. I felt lost with tears in my eyes. I just wanted to sign up for school. I didn't need pity—I needed direction. This time, I was met with warmth. A Native American job counselor by the name of Deb Eagle greeted me with respect. She spoke like she had grown up with people like me. Familiar rhythm, shared experience. She saw my eyes, wet and tired, and after explaining everything I went through, she said gently, "I'm sorry you were treated that way."

She didn't rush. She didn't redirect. She listened.

And just like that, I felt like my dignity returned.

That first office had left me shaken. Sitting across from that lady in that sea of cubicles, I remember thinking, this is supposed to be someone who helps people. Instead, her flat tone and clipped questions made me feel like I was a problem she wanted to get rid of. I had never been treated like that before in a professional setting, and it hit me hard. Where I grew up, we often had to teach people how to treat us—but in that moment, I felt the sting of being reduced to a checkbox.

And when she called me later to reroute me to "the center for people of color," I felt my chest tighten. In my community, "people of color" was not a phrase we used with each other but hearing it from her lips in that context sounded more like "colored people." Outdated. Dismissive. Another reminder of how words can carry weight when they come from someone who doesn't see you.

But then came Deb Eagle. Her body language alone was different—inviting, calm. Her tone was soft but strong, educated but lived-in. She listened like she actually understood. She reminded me of an auntie, someone protective, someone who had experienced some of my same challenges. In that cubicle, I felt something return that the other woman had tried to strip away: my dignity.

Deb didn't just help me in that moment. She spoke my name in rooms I hadn't yet entered. She advocated for me where I didn't even know I needed advocating. Later, when I became a manager in the same program, I heard how highly she had spoken of me all along. She believed in me before I could believe in myself. And at that very first meeting, she gave me what I had been begging for all along—not pity, not handouts, but direction. Respect. A clear next step.

That's what dignity looks like when systems try to strip it from you and someone else restores it. One counselor saw me as a burden. Another saw me as a person. Theory calls that bias, microaggressions, counterspace—but to me, it was lived reality. One "no" tried to erase me. One "yes" reminded me I belonged.

Theory in Practice: The Cost of Dismissal

Maslow's Hierarchy—Esteem & Belonging (Maslow, 1943, p. 382):

I was seeking tools to elevate myself—education, opportunity. But the first counselor denied esteem and belonging. The last one gave it freely, and it made all the difference.

Erikson's Industry vs. Inferiority (Erikson, 1963, p. 27):

I was trying to demonstrate capability, to claim competence. The system tried to reinforce inferiority through low expectations and coded dismissal. I pushed back—and preserved my industry.

Attachment Theory — Belonging and Worth (Bowlby, 1982; Bretherton, 1992):

Discrimination distorts attachment; it tells children they don't belong where they stand. But adult healing rebuilds secure bonds—with self, with culture, with community—one affirmation at a time.

Lessons From That Office Door

I didn't walk in asking for permission. I walked in asking for a pathway. The first counselor tried to reroute me. Box me in. The last counselor simply said: Let's figure this out.

In that moment, I realized something vital: Help isn't help if it comes without dignity. And dignity isn't a gift—it's a fight.

Discussion Questions

1. How do Maslow's concepts of esteem and belonging shape educational access?
2. In what ways does Erikson's stage of industry vs. inferiority show up in adult reentry and career decisions?
3. How might structural racism influence perceived capability and career pathways?
4. What happens when gatekeepers fail to see clients as full people?
5. Reflect on a moment when someone offered help without respect. How did you respond—and what changed in you?

Comparative Overview of Human Development and Attachment Theories

Figure 1.1

Sigmund Freud's Psychosexual Stages of Development

Stage	Age Range	Erogenous Zone	Developmental Descriptions
Oral	Birth – 1 year	Mouth	Sucking, biting
Anal	1 – 3 years	Anus	Toilet training
Phallic	3 – 6 years	Genital	Identity with same-sex parent
Latency	6 – 12 years	Dormant	Socialization
Genitals	12+ years	Genitals	Intimacy, reflection

Figure 1.2

Lawrence Kohlberg's Stages of Moral Development

Levels	Age Range	Stage
Pre-conventional	3 – 7 years	Obedience and Punishment
Conventional	8 – 13 years	Social Approval and Law & Order
Post-conventional	13+ years	Social Contract and Universal Ethics

Figure 1.3

Jean Piaget's Cognitive Development of Moral Development

Stage	Age Range	Developmental Descriptions
Sensorimotor	Birth–2 years	Senses and Motor Coordination
Preoperational	2–7 years	Symbolic Thinking
Concrete Operational	7–11 years	Logic with Concrete Objects
Formal Operational	11+ years	Abstract Reason

Figure 1.4

Erik Erikson Psychosocial Stages of Development

Stage	Age Range	Developmental Descriptions
Infancy	Birth–1 year	Trust vs. Mistrust
Early Childhood	1–3 years	Autonomy vs. Shame/Doubt
Preschool	3–6 years	Initiative vs. Guilt
School Age	6–12 years	Industry vs. Inferiority
Adolescent	12–18 years	Identity vs. Role Confusion
Young Adulthood	18–40 years	Intimacy vs. Isolation
Middle Adulthood	40–65 years	Generativity vs. Stagnation
Maturity	65+ years	Ego Integrity vs. Despair

Comparative Overview of Human Development and Attachment Theories

Figure 2.1
Abraham Maslow's Hierarchy of Needs

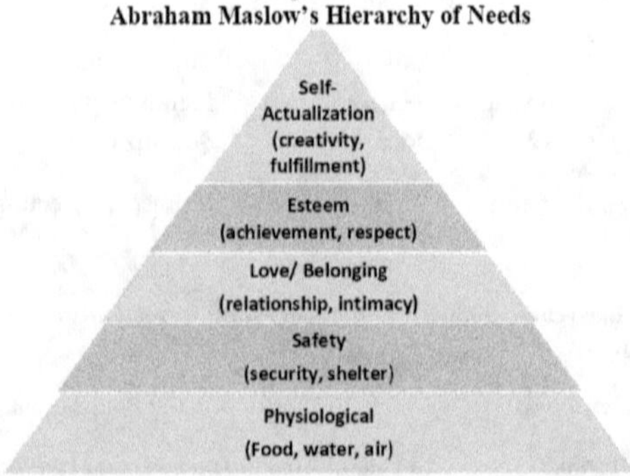

Figure 2.2
John Bowlby's Four Phases of Attachment

Phase	Age Range	Description
Pre-attachment	Birth-6 weeks	Infants show no specific attachment; respond to anyone.
Attachment-in-the-making	6 weeks - 6/8 months	Infants begin to prefer familiar caregivers; build trust.
Clear-cut attachment	6/8 months – 18/24 months	Strong attachment forms: separation anxiety and protest emerge.
Formation of reciprocal relationships	18/24 months +	Child understands caregiver's comings/goings; communication improves.

Figure 2.3
Mary Ainsworth's Attachment Syles (Strange Situation)

Attachment Styles	Behavior During Separation & Reunion
Secure	Distressed when caregiver leaves; easily comforted upon return.
Insecure-Avoidant	Shows little distress; avoids caregiver upon return.
Insecure-Resistant (ambivalent)	Very distressed; seeks contact but resists comfort. Clingy and hard to soothe.
Disorganized	Confused, fearful, or contradictory behavior. Often linked to trauma or neglect.

CHAPTER 17

Ground-Level Grace

Theme: Advocacy isn't a job—it's a return to the places that raised you.

When Deb looked at the Human Services program form I brought in, she didn't flinch, squint, or try to redirect me. She said plainly, "If this is the program you want to take, we'll figure out how to get you signed up." That sentence wrapped around my ribs like armor. We ended up going through the vocational rehabilitation program, and they helped me with getting signed up for school.

I started the program the next semester. And just like that—my world shifted.

I got offered a full role as an Employment Advocate at the center. A job that mattered. A job that paid. And I ran with it. But this moment didn't fall out of the sky. It came from grind. It came from walking into systems designed to turn me away—and staying long enough for them to see me elevate. It came from saying yes to myself when no one else would. By then, Deb was the manager of the program.

Walking into my first class felt like my journey was just beginning. I didn't know how it would end, but I knew I was ready. The instructor of the Human Services program also taught many of my classes, and the way she broke things down stuck with me immediately. This program laid the very foundation for everything that I learned in my social work programs. The classroom itself felt inviting, the kind of place where you could breathe and still believe in possibility. I remember times this instructor would allow me to bring my child into class to accommodate life circumstances that showed up out of nowhere. For the first time, I could picture telling my kids one day, Mama didn't just survive—she went to school and made something of herself.

I threw myself into it all—school full time, work full time, and being a mom full time. The weight was heavy, but the support around me kept me moving. Deb. My family. Even the school itself. They allowed me to bring my kids when something unexpected happened. Sometimes they sat in the back of class, sometimes with me at work. Those small accommodations were lifesavers. My kids may never fully know how much that grace carried me, but without it, I don't know how I would have kept going.

When I stepped into the role of Employment Advocate, it wasn't about checking boxes, it was about restoring breath to people who were drowning in the same storm I once came through. I didn't sit in my office pushing papers around. I hit the pavement. I was in the Grocery stores, shelters, interview drop-offs—I was in it. My car felt more like a mobile intervention site than transportation.

Advocacy felt like slipping into a second skin. I didn't need training to understand the people they called "high-risk." I had been one of them. Families with nothing—no home, no food, no clothes, dealing with Child Protection, domestic violence, addiction, unemployment. I knew that reality because I had lived it.

People needed more than job referrals—they needed someone who saw them, stood beside them, and reminded them they weren't invisible.

Being an Employment Advocate while studying made everything click faster. What I learned in the classroom, I practiced in real time. What I lived in the field, I brought back into the classroom. Helping people who were right where I once had been was natural. I looked them in the eyes and told them; I wasn't always in this chair. I've been where you are. You can get through this too. I didn't just hand out referrals. I handed out hope, motivation, and resources I knew could change the course of a life.

I finished my Human Service program in two years with honors and earned my associate's degree at WITC, in Superior, WI. Graduation came after two years, but it felt like a lifetime of climbing. When I walked across that stage and held my associate's degree in my hands, it wasn't just paper. It was proof that I hadn't stopped at survival. It gave me motivation to keep pressing forward. My kids were the reason I crossed that finish line—every late night, every class, every moment I wanted to quit. They deserved to see what was possible. They deserved a mother who didn't just say, you can become more but showed them.

That's what real advocacy looks like—lifting others while you're still climbing yourself. Theory calls it peer support, experiential knowledge, human-centered practice. But for me, it was ground-level grace: turning my lived experience into proof that rising is possible.

Theory in Practice: Advocacy Rooted in Experience

Maslow's Hierarchy—Safety Before Strategy (Maslow, 1943):

No job program works if you ignore food, shelter, safety. Before people can think about employment or goals, they need to be warm, fed, and safe. I understood that deeply because I'd been in survival mode myself.

Erikson's Industry vs. Inferiority (Erikson, 1963):

Most of my participants were stuck somewhere between mistrust and shame, not because they weren't trying but because the world kept throwing punches before they even had a chance. My job was to help them remember who they were—competent, worthy, capable.

Bowlby's Attachment Theory — Safety as Foundation (Bowlby, 1982; Bretherton, 1992):

My background wasn't baggage—it was the blueprint. The bonds I lost and rebuilt taught me how safety shapes survival. Every family I helped echoed that first lesson—that healing begins where connection returns.

Lessons From the Pavement

I never saw this work as a climb up the ladder—I saw it as a walk back down to lift others up. There were moments—raw, unforgettable ones—where someone's story cracked me wide open. A young mother juggling too much with too little. A teen who had fire in his eyes but no one to fan the flame. Those stories didn't just haunt me, they moved me.

And they reminded me: I wasn't just working. I was testifying.

Discussion Questions

1. How does staying connected to your origin story shape your leadership?
2. Can personal experience elevate professional advocacy, or does it blur boundaries?
3. How do systems define "high-risk"—and what impact does that label have on real people?
4. How can staying emotionally connected to the communities we serve influence systems-level change?
5. What does it look like to honor your lived experience while holding space for someone else's journey, especially when they're still in the storm?

Comparative Overview of Human Development and Attachment Theories

Figure 1.1

Sigmund Freud's Psychosexual Stages of Development

Stage	Age Range	Erogenous Zone	Developmental Descriptions
Oral	Birth – 1 year	Mouth	Sucking, biting
Anal	1 – 3 years	Anus	Toilet training
Phallic	3 – 6 years	Genital	Identity with same-sex parent
Latency	6 – 12 years	Dormant	Socialization
Genitals	12+ years	Genitals	Intimacy, reflection

Figure 1.2

Lawrence Kohlberg's Stages of Moral Development

Levels	Age Range	Stage
Pre-conventional	3 – 7 years	Obedience and Punishment
Conventional	8 – 13 years	Social Approval and Law & Order
Post-conventional	13+ years	Social Contract and Universal Ethics

Figure 1.3

Jean Piaget's Cognitive Development of Moral Development

Stage	Age Range	Developmental Descriptions
Sensorimotor	Birth–2 years	Senses and Motor Coordination
Preoperational	2–7 years	Symbolic Thinking
Concrete Operational	7–11 years	Logic with Concrete Objects
Formal Operational	11+ years	Abstract Reason

Figure 1.4

Erik Erikson Psychosocial Stages of Development

Stage	Age Range	Developmental Descriptions
Infancy	Birth–1 year	Trust vs. Mistrust
Early Childhood	1–3 years	Autonomy vs. Shame/Doubt
Preschool	3–6 years	Initiative vs. Guilt
School Age	6–12 years	Industry vs. Inferiority
Adolescent	12–18 years	Identity vs. Role Confusion
Young Adulthood	18–40 years	Intimacy vs. Isolation
Middle Adulthood	40–65 years	Generativity vs. Stagnation
Maturity	65+ years	Ego Integrity vs. Despair

Comparative Overview of Human Development and Attachment Theories

Figure 2.1
Abraham Maslow's Hierarchy of Needs

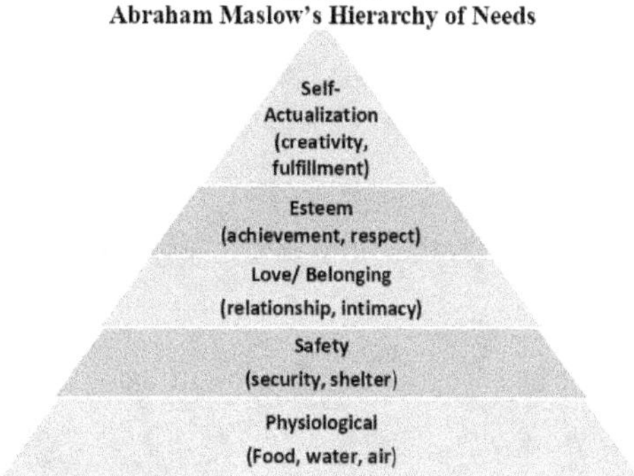

Figure 2.2
John Bowlby's Four Phases of Attachment

Phase	Age Range	Description
Pre-attachment	Birth-6 weeks	Infants show no specific attachment; respond to anyone.
Attachment-in-the-making	6 weeks - 6/8 months	Infants begin to prefer familiar caregivers; build trust.
Clear-cut attachment	6/8 months – 18/24 months	Strong attachment forms: separation anxiety and protest emerge.
Formation of reciprocal relationships	18/24 months +	Child understands caregiver's comings/goings; communication improves.

Figure 2.3
Mary Ainsworth's Attachment Syles (Strange Situation)

Attachment Styles	Behavior During Separation & Reunion
Secure	Distressed when caregiver leaves; easily comforted upon return.
Insecure-Avoidant	Shows little distress; avoids caregiver upon return.
Insecure-Resistant (ambivalent)	Very distressed; seeks contact but resists comfort. Clingy and hard to soothe.
Disorganized	Confused, fearful, or contradictory behavior. Often linked to trauma or neglect.

CHAPTER 18

Front Row at My Own Revolution

Theme: Nobody handed me a seat—I built the damn table and sent out invitations.

After I received my associates degree, I applied and was accepted into the Social Work program for my bachelor's degree.

I applied for and was offered the job counselor position at the Center. I was so excited about how my life was elevating. There's a flavor of freedom that's hard to describe. You feel it in your bones. In the bills that get paid on time. In the extra twenty for cleats or dance tights. In the way your kids walk into practice or rehearsal with confidence because they know Mama came through.

As a job counselor, I had to attend the same quarterly meetings as all the other job counselors, including Tawnya, the job counselor who I had the first encounter with, the one who once dismissed me like I was a burden on her clipboard. There was a bit of a rush knowing I was about to be in the same room as her. On the day of the meeting, she saw me walk in wearing her same job title. I was excited but remained humble. Our eyes connected when I walked in the room. She blinked. I didn't.

Walking into those quarterly meetings and sitting across from Tawnya wasn't about rubbing anything in her face. It was about reclaiming something I thought I had lost in her office years before. Back then, she left me feeling defeated. Now, with the same job title beside my name, the victory was mine. I had beat her perception of me. More importantly, I had beat the voice in my own head that once said, maybe she's right.

After an additional two years, I completed the social work program and earned my bachelor's degree. I graduated summa cum Laude. I often looked back on my life and wondered how I did it. I was proud of myself. I didn't have words for how I felt. I couldn't describe the work that I put in. I knew I was doing it for my children and for me. I thought to myself, what if I could get my master's degree?

My counselor at the vocational program informed me that because I had graduated at the top of my class in both my associate's and bachelor's program, they would pay for me to do my master's program, which they didn't do often. This was all the confirmation I needed since I had already been thinking about this.

After I applied for the social work program for my master's degree, I got accepted and was able to enter a scholar program with a focus on child welfare.

While taking my grad classes, I applied and was offered a management position of the employment services program at the center. Deb, my mentor and former supervisor relocated. I was excited to accept this position.

When I stepped into management, I chose to keep a caseload. This was unusual for a program manager, but it was intentional. I wasn't about to lose touch just because my title changed. I'd sat in too many meetings where managers talked about participants like they were just numbers—grant metrics, spreadsheet codes, nothing personal. I couldn't stomach it. Those participants were me once.

I needed to keep my feet on the ground, so I never forgot where I came from. It was important for me to be an example for my children and their future. I needed them to see what that connection looked like. I wanted to model what it meant to rise without losing your roots.

It wasn't until after I became program manager that Tawnya, the job counselor that essentially turned me away, eventually came over to speak. That moment didn't need fire—it needed grace sharpened with memory. When she came over, I didn't snap. I didn't snub. I met her with poise. My words were measured, warm, professional. But make no mistake—I remembered everything.

I often think about how the very person who tried to deny me a path that I wanted to build for me and my family, and who told me that I wouldn't make more than nine or ten dollars after completing the human service associates' program, would be able to see that same person surpass her position. This was a moment.

After a year and a half, I completed the scholar program and obtained my Master of Social Work Degree. I graduated cum laude, top of my class again.

That degree didn't just validate me—it repositioned me.

What I didn't realize was that every test I passed, every paper I turned in, every shift I worked—it wasn't just for me. It was for my kids. For the extra money that got my daughter into performing arts school. For the football fees that kept my sons busy throughout the day. For the ability to say "yes" instead of "I'm sorry, baby. We can't."

My husband and I got married a few months before I received my bachelor's degree. We had our last child just a few months after we tied the knot. After sixteen years of being together, we decided it was past time. We didn't see the need to before. We knew we were committed to each other. My husband worked as an electrical engineer, while I continued my grad program and worked at the Center. We had finally built something stable—and I knew exactly what it had cost to get there.

Graduation ceremonies became sacred markers. For my bachelor's, I stood with a gold cord around my neck, my robe draped over a dress that made me feel strong, and my name was echoing in a hall filled with my family, my husband, my kids, my mom, my dad and my sisters, even my uncle. Their cheers wrapped around me like a blanket. By the time I earned my master's, the cord had changed to silver, but the pride was just as heavy in my chest. I looked out into the audience, breathed in the moment, and silently thanked God for carrying me.

The grind to get there was not glamorous. I wrote papers with nausea creeping up my throat, deadlines pressing in before midnight, and exhaustion tugging at my body. Pregnancy didn't pause because school was demanding. Motherhood didn't wait because I had assignments. But quitting was never on the table. My kids deserved to watch me finish. They needed to see that even in discomfort, you can carry things through.

Marriage became another layer of that testimony. Sixteen years of ups and downs had taught us survival, but standing at the altar sealed it. Our last child was on the way, and we laughed about how it took our final pregnancy to finally push us there. Our marriage hasn't been perfect—it's been tested, stretched, and bent—but it has endured. Looking back on our history, we sometimes shake our heads at what we once thought was normal. But those very moments became lessons. We turned our mistakes into warnings, our growth into examples. Our kids may roll their eyes when we start in, but later they circle back with, "Mom, Dad, you were right."

What we built together was more than a marriage certificate—it was a family story with roots deep enough to hold us steady. We had weathered so much: poverty, prison, probation, disappointment. Yet there we were, raising children who had stability where we once had struggle. We still had our arguments, our quiet stretches of silent treatments, but we also had laughter around dinner tables, family vacations, family gatherings, kids running in and out of rooms, and a kind of trust that only comes from walking through fire together. Our marriage gave our children something to lean on, but it also gave us a mirror to see how far we'd come.

This stage of life taught me that rising isn't about outpacing others—it's about refusing to shrink into the boxes they try to put you in. I wasn't just surviving anymore. I was building stability, building legacy, building proof that I had never been a statistic—I was a story being rewritten.

This is what resilience looks like when it grows up: It stops being about proving people wrong and becomes about building spaces for others to rise, too. Theory names its self-determination, counter-narrative, resistance. I call it my revolution—front row at a table I built alongside my husband, with seats for my children right beside us.

Theory in Practice: The Anatomy of a Rise

Maslow's Self-Actualization (Maslow, 1943, p. 382):

There are points in my life where I hit the top of the pyramid—and there are times when I've had to discover myself again after life happens, but I never doubt finding my way back because I never stop climbing when the stairs got slick.

Erikson's Generativity vs. Stagnation (Erikson, 1963, p. 26):

I'm in the season of giving back—building systems that work better than the ones I came through.

Bowlby's Attachment Theory (Bowlby, 1982; Bretherton, 1992):

Attachment was my first education. Bowlby showed me how secure bonds shape the courage to explore. Education was my tool, not just my trophy. I'm teaching through existence—every connection, every role, every child I protect reinforces that safety expands learning.

Lessons From the Front Line

I used to sit outside institutions longing for entry. Now I help to shape what it looks like for people—and how they're treated when they arrive. My rise wasn't just personal. It's proof of possibility. Proof that grit, grace, and a whole lot of grind can rewrite generational patterns.

And I'm not done yet.

Discussion Questions

1. How does education function as both escape and empowerment in cycles of poverty?
2. In what ways does grace serve as resistance when facing old systems of dismissal?
3. How can theory (Maslow, Erikson's, Freire) help us frame long-term transformation?
4. What emotional complexities arise when confronting past gatekeepers as a peer or superior?
5. Reflect on a time when financial freedom altered not just your lifestyle—but your identity. What changed?

Comparative Overview of Human Development and Attachment Theories

Figure 1.1

Sigmund Freud's Psychosexual Stages of Development

Stage	Age Range	Erogenous Zone	Developmental Descriptions
Oral	Birth – 1 year	Mouth	Sucking, biting
Anal	1 – 3 years	Anus	Toilet training
Phallic	3 – 6 years	Genital	Identity with same-sex parent
Latency	6 – 12 years	Dormant	Socialization
Genitals	12+ years	Genitals	Intimacy, reflection

Figure 1.2

Lawrence Kohlberg's Stages of Moral Development

Levels	Age Range	Stage
Pre-conventional	3 – 7 years	Obedience and Punishment
Conventional	8 – 13 years	Social Approval and Law & Order
Post-conventional	13+ years	Social Contract and Universal Ethics

Figure 1.3

Jean Piaget's Cognitive Development of Moral Development

Stage	Age Range	Developmental Descriptions
Sensorimotor	Birth–2 years	Senses and Motor Coordination
Preoperational	2–7 years	Symbolic Thinking
Concrete Operational	7–11 years	Logic with Concrete Objects
Formal Operational	11+ years	Abstract Reason

Figure 1.4

Erik Erikson Psychosocial Stages of Development

Stage	Age Range	Developmental Descriptions
Infancy	Birth–1 year	Trust vs. Mistrust
Early Childhood	1–3 years	Autonomy vs. Shame/Doubt
Preschool	3–6 years	Initiative vs. Guilt
School Age	6–12 years	Industry vs. Inferiority
Adolescent	12–18 years	Identity vs. Role Confusion
Young Adulthood	18–40 years	Intimacy vs. Isolation
Middle Adulthood	40–65 years	Generativity vs. Stagnation
Maturity	65+ years	Ego Integrity vs. Despair

Comparative Overview
of Human Development and Attachment Theories

Figure 2.1
Abraham Maslow's Hierarchy of Needs

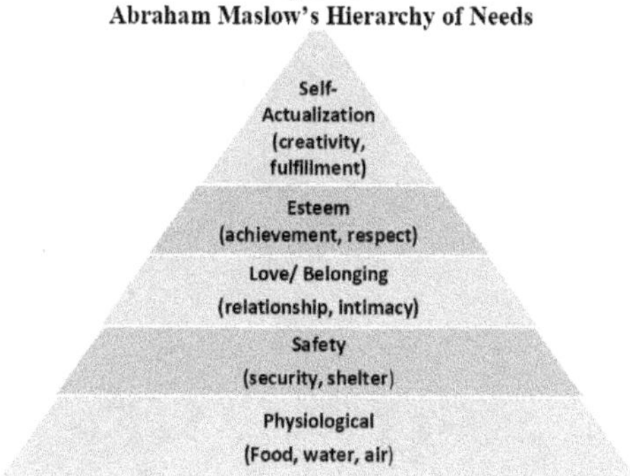

Figure 2.2
John Bowlby's Four Phases of Attachment

Phase	Age Range	Description
Pre-attachment	Birth-6 weeks	Infants show no specific attachment; respond to anyone.
Attachment-in-the-making	6 weeks - 6/8 months	Infants begin to prefer familiar caregivers; build trust.
Clear-cut attachment	6/8 months – 18/24 months	Strong attachment forms: separation anxiety and protest emerge.
Formation of reciprocal relationships	18/24 months +	Child understands caregiver's comings/goings; communication improves.

Figure 2.3
Mary Ainsworth's Attachment Syles (Strange Situation)

Attachment Styles	Behavior During Separation & Reunion
Secure	Distressed when caregiver leaves; easily comforted upon return.
Insecure-Avoidant	Shows little distress; avoids caregiver upon return.
Insecure-Resistant (ambivalent)	Very distressed; seeks contact but resists comfort. Clingy and hard to soothe.
Disorganized	Confused, fearful, or contradictory behavior. Often linked to trauma or neglect.

CHAPTER 19

Still Standing, Still Serving

Theme: From being the case to carrying them—this is what full circle looks like.

I know what it's like to be denied. Not just a good job or a lease for an apartment—but dignity. As a convicted felon who spent time in jail, prison, and a halfway house, I've stared into eyes that had already decided that I wasn't worth the risk. The label follows you like a shadow—especially when you're trying to rise.

But by the grace of God, my conviction records were expunged after all of the hard work I put in to become who I am today. Not because the system suddenly got generous—but because my growth as a citizen spoke louder than my past. And the timing? God lined it up perfect. The period that needed to pass before I could get my background convictions expunged aligned right up with the timing that it took for me to obtain my master's degree. The judge ordered the expungements a few months before I graduated. That wasn't a coincidence. That was God.

When the judge cleared my record, I stood there proud. Not just because he spoke on my accomplishments, but because I could finally speak pride over myself. That little girl who once chased her daddy out the door was now chasing her dreams. That moment was more than legal relief—it was personal redemption. Nobody gave me that. I fought for it, and I will protect it at all costs, because only I know the weight it took to get here.

Once my record was expunged, I was able to apply to the job I went to school for. My goal, as a Child Welfare Scholar, is to work in the field.

I applied and was accepted for a social worker position in the child protection department at an agency near our home. Although I wanted to thrive in this position, it was too stressful. The workplace culture mimicked the same experience that I received from that first job counselor who also worked in the same building as I did, just in a different department.

It was so bad that I needed to seek therapy for some of the racism that I was experiencing. I found myself needing to file grievances and sitting in meetings more times than I ever wanted to. I was one of two African American social workers in the unit that I worked in. The other African American social worker who worked there years before me, describes it as having to go through a hazing process as a person of color. She left that job as well. The work environment was too hostile for me, and I had to look for another job.

I stayed there for about a year and a half, and then I started looking for another job. I applied for a social worker position closer to the city I grew up in and was offered the job. My oldest child and only daughter had moved closer to the city as well about six months prior. She blessed me with two beautiful grandchildren at that time, and I wanted more than anything to be close to them. So, when I obtained the job, it worked out well. More diversity and people who look like me.

I was able to provide meaningful service at my new job. I was a lot more relaxed. I felt more supported. My job felt more natural. I also provided meaningful services in my prior child protection position as well, but the hostile work environment made it difficult for me to show up as my whole-self for the clients that I worked with. This didn't sit right with me, even though my clients couldn't tell. I wanted to feel like I could be comfortable at work, so that I could show up for my clients. I knew that it was important to have moments of clarity and self-awareness in this field due to the burn-out that could have happened if I didn't check myself.

Even with my record expunged, degrees in hand, and new titles behind my name, I still couldn't escape a truth: Racism is real, and it is alive. It is embedded in policies, laws, and everyday practices that pass themselves off as "standard procedure." It's not limited to one county or one office; it's institutional, structural, and historical. This is what many call systemic racism, but I've lived it. I've felt it in different places, in the silence of colleagues who looked the other way while I struggled under the weight of it. That silence is its own form of violence.

And here's where my conviction sits: I don't fault people for being born into racist systems. But when you recognize it and do nothing—that's complicity. When you catch yourself contributing to bias and choose comfort instead of change—that's how racism breathes generation after generation. Systems don't shift on their own. People shift them. And those of us in the helping profession have a moral responsibility to confront what we see, not just in policy but in practice.

That's why it felt different at my new job. The policies were the same, but the people showed up differently. There, I felt supported, I felt seen, I felt I could bring my whole self into the work. That shift allowed me to serve families more fully, without the split of hiding part of myself to survive the environment.

During this time, I decided it was time for me to buy a home, instead of renting. I was on housing assistance for the past eight years. I was considered poverty level due to the amount of money I made and the size of my family. That assistance helped me so much. It gave me a chance to save up enough money for a down payment on a home. I wanted to create generational wealth for my children. We were approved for a home loan, and we moved into our home a month after I started my new position at my new job as a social worker.

Buying my first home was another turning point. Walking through that door with my children and knowing it was ours—that moment planted roots deeper than poverty could reach. It wasn't just about shelter. It was about creating generational wealth, laying a foundation that my children could stand on.

What is interesting is that a short time after I came home from prison, I obtained custody of my niece due to her experiencing something no little girl should ever have to go through. Something that was all too familiar. For a short time, I was her foster mom. As a little girl myself, I was also involved in the child welfare system.

Let that land: I grew up in foster homes, and now I was able to provide safety and security. When I became a child protection worker, I figured out early that I don't think I chose to be in this field, I honestly believe it chose me. I'd gone from being the file on someone's desk to guiding parents through systems I once lived in. There's no theory in this. It's my real life. It's full circle with a heartbeat.

Taking in my niece carried the same kind of full-circle weight. I had once been the child shuffled through placements, the file on someone else's desk. And now, I was the one offering safety, making sure another little girl didn't feel what I once felt. That is lived experience turned into service. That is what it means when I say I didn't choose this field—it chose me.

This is the part where theory and testimony meet. Social work names it systemic oppression, institutional racism, restorative practice. But I know it as survival, as resilience, as serving from scars that healed into strength. I've gone from being the case to carrying the case.

Theory in Practice: From Surviving to Protecting

Erikson's Generativity vs. Stagnation (Erikson, 1963):

I chose legacy. I chose service. I rejected stagnation in favor of building something that outlasts my own pain.

Maslow's Self – Actualization (Maslow, 1943):

I reached a place of fulfillment—educating, advocating, and protecting others. My alignment of healing, faith, and professional achievement speaks to wholeness.

Attachment Theory—Secure Base Reversed (Bowlby, 1982; Bretherton, 1992):

I became a secure base for my niece during her trauma. That act rewrote the narrative—not just hers but mine too.

Lessons From the Other Side of the Desk

I walk into work knowing exactly what it costs to ask for help. I remember being the one everyone doubted. And now, I'm the one families' trust. That isn't just justice. That's healing. That's purpose with a badge and a backbone.

Every family I serve carries a thread of my own story. And every time I advocate, protect, or simply listen—I'm not just working. I'm testifying.

Discussion Questions

1. How does personal experience with trauma or systemic barriers inform ethical practice in helping professions?
2. What role does timing—both spiritual and logistical—play in narratives of transformation?
3. In what ways can former system-involved individuals serve as reformers within those same systems?
4. How do moments of "full circle" contribute to the emotional and professional clarity of a person's mission?
5. What does it mean to carry a legacy that once carried you?

Comparative Overview
of Human Development and Attachment Theories

Figure 1.1

Sigmund Freud's Psychosexual Stages of Development

Stage	Age Range	Erogenous Zone	Developmental Descriptions
Oral	Birth – 1 year	Mouth	Sucking, biting
Anal	1 – 3 years	Anus	Toilet training
Phallic	3 – 6 years	Genital	Identity with same-sex parent
Latency	6 – 12 years	Dormant	Socialization
Genitals	12+ years	Genitals	Intimacy, reflection

Figure 1.2

Lawrence Kohlberg's Stages of Moral Development

Levels	Age Range	Stage
Pre-conventional	3 – 7 years	Obedience and Punishment
Conventional	8 – 13 years	Social Approval and Law & Order
Post-conventional	13+ years	Social Contract and Universal Ethics

Figure 1.3

Jean Piaget's Cognitive Development of Moral Development

Stage	Age Range	Developmental Descriptions
Sensorimotor	Birth–2 years	Senses and Motor Coordination
Preoperational	2–7 years	Symbolic Thinking
Concrete Operational	7–11 years	Logic with Concrete Objects
Formal Operational	11+ years	Abstract Reason

Figure 1.4

Erik Erikson Psychosocial Stages of Development

Stage	Age Range	Developmental Descriptions
Infancy	Birth–1 year	Trust vs. Mistrust
Early Childhood	1–3 years	Autonomy vs. Shame/Doubt
Preschool	3–6 years	Initiative vs. Guilt
School Age	6–12 years	Industry vs. Inferiority
Adolescent	12–18 years	Identity vs. Role Confusion
Young Adulthood	18–40 years	Intimacy vs. Isolation
Middle Adulthood	40–65 years	Generativity vs. Stagnation
Maturity	65+ years	Ego Integrity vs. Despair

Comparative Overview of Human Development and Attachment Theories

Figure 2.1
Abraham Maslow's Hierarchy of Needs

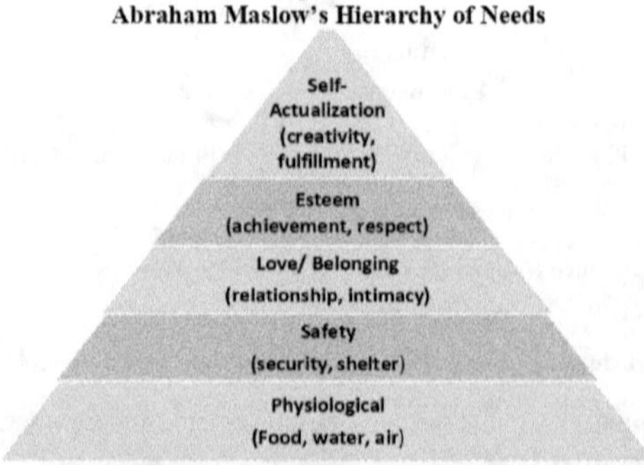

Figure 2.2
John Bowlby's Four Phases of Attachment

Phase	Age Range	Description
Pre-attachment	Birth-6 weeks	Infants show no specific attachment; respond to anyone.
Attachment-in-the-making	6 weeks - 6/8 months	Infants begin to prefer familiar caregivers; build trust.
Clear-cut attachment	6/8 months – 18/24 months	Strong attachment forms: separation anxiety and protest emerge.
Formation of reciprocal relationships	18/24 months +	Child understands caregiver's comings/goings; communication improves.

Figure 2.3
Mary Ainsworth's Attachment Syles (Strange Situation)

Attachment Styles	Behavior During Separation & Reunion
Secure	Distressed when caregiver leaves; easily comforted upon return.
Insecure-Avoidant	Shows little distress; avoids caregiver upon return.
Insecure-Resistant (ambivalent)	Very distressed; seeks contact but resists comfort. Clingy and hard to soothe.
Disorganized	Confused, fearful, or contradictory behavior. Often linked to trauma or neglect.

CHAPTER 20

The Legacy I Carry

Theme: Some stories aren't just meant to be told—they're meant to teach.

I've learned that survival isn't the whole story. It's the prologue. The real story is what you build after. The legacy. The blueprint. The truth you leave behind for someone else to follow.

This book isn't just about what happened to me—it's about what I did with it. From foster homes to prison cells, courtrooms to classrooms, every chapter has a message. Every scar has a theory behind it. And every rise has a blueprint someone else can use.

I didn't write this to relive my past. I wrote it to reframe it. To show students, educators, and survivors that trauma doesn't get the final say. That developmental theory isn't just academic—it's lived. That healing is possible, even when the odds say otherwise.

My children will grow up knowing exactly who their mother was. Where she came from. What she overcame. And how she broke cycles that once seemed infinite. They'll know that grit and grace can coexist. That pain can be turned into purpose. That legacy isn't just what you leave—it's what you live.

I offer this book not just as testimony—but as tool. For psychology classrooms. For social work students. For system-involved parents. For anyone who needs to know that redemption is more than just a church word—it's a process with fingerprints on it.

I walked through systems that were never built for my healing. And now I work inside them, building something better.

The legacy I carry is layered—with theory, conviction, and the kind of truth you only get from living it.

Theory in Practice: Integration and Impact

Erikson's Psychosocial Stages:

From mistrust to generativity, I've lived every stage. Not in perfect order but in real time. My identity was fractured and reformed. My roles shifted from client to protector. My purpose now lives in service.

Maslow's Hierarchy—From Safety to Self-Actualization:

I climbed from the bottom—housing insecurity, emotional instability, survival mode—and reached my version of the top. Not because I had everything but because I built something meaningful from what I had.

Attachment Theory—Repair and Reconnection:

My relationships with my children, my niece, and even my parents reflect the possibility of healing. Secure attachment isn't just built—it can be rebuilt. And I'm living proof.

Lessons From a Life Rewritten

I used to measure growth by what I had: degrees, promotions, records expunged. Now, I measure it by what I give. Protection. Support. Opportunity. I've learned that healing isn't always linear—but it's always possible when you decide your story is worth telling.

This memoir is my offering. My curriculum. My legacy.

Discussion Questions

1. How can memoirs function as curriculum in higher education?
2. What makes lived experience a credible lens for analyzing developmental theory?
3. How does transformation within systems (like foster care or incarceration) alter the system itself?
4. What do legacy and healing mean to those who grew up in instability?
5. How can storytelling become a tool for both personal and collective change?

Comparative Overview of Human Development and Attachment Theories

Figure 1.1

Sigmund Freud's Psychosexual Stages of Development

Stage	Age Range	Erogenous Zone	Developmental Descriptions
Oral	Birth – 1 year	Mouth	Sucking, biting
Anal	1 – 3 years	Anus	Toilet training
Phallic	3 – 6 years	Genital	Identity with same-sex parent
Latency	6 – 12 years	Dormant	Socialization
Genitals	12+ years	Genitals	Intimacy, reflection

Figure 1.2

Lawrence Kohlberg's Stages of Moral Development

Levels	Age Range	Stage
Pre-conventional	3 – 7 years	Obedience and Punishment
Conventional	8 – 13 years	Social Approval and Law & Order
Post-conventional	13+ years	Social Contract and Universal Ethics

Figure 1.3

Jean Piaget's Cognitive Development of Moral Development

Stage	Age Range	Developmental Descriptions
Sensorimotor	Birth–2 years	Senses and Motor Coordination
Preoperational	2–7 years	Symbolic Thinking
Concrete Operational	7–11 years	Logic with Concrete Objects
Formal Operational	11+ years	Abstract Reason

Figure 1.4

Erik Erikson Psychosocial Stages of Development

Stage	Age Range	Developmental Descriptions
Infancy	Birth–1 year	Trust vs. Mistrust
Early Childhood	1–3 years	Autonomy vs. Shame/Doubt
Preschool	3–6 years	Initiative vs. Guilt
School Age	6–12 years	Industry vs. Inferiority
Adolescent	12–18 years	Identity vs. Role Confusion
Young Adulthood	18–40 years	Intimacy vs. Isolation
Middle Adulthood	40–65 years	Generativity vs. Stagnation
Maturity	65+ years	Ego Integrity vs. Despair

Comparative Overview of Human Development and Attachment Theories

Figure 2.1
Abraham Maslow's Hierarchy of Needs

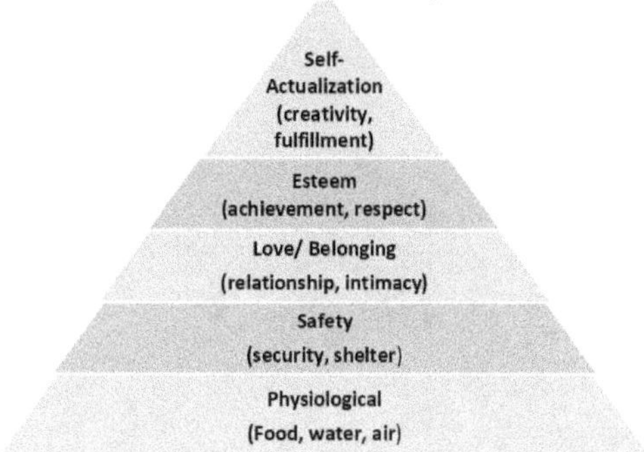

Figure 2.2
John Bowlby's Four Phases of Attachment

Phase	Age Range	Description
Pre-attachment	Birth-6 weeks	Infants show no specific attachment; respond to anyone.
Attachment-in-the-making	6 weeks - 6/8 months	Infants begin to prefer familiar caregivers; build trust.
Clear-cut attachment	6/8 months – 18/24 months	Strong attachment forms: separation anxiety and protest emerge.
Formation of reciprocal relationships	18/24 months +	Child understands caregiver's comings/goings; communication improves.

Figure 2.3
Mary Ainsworth's Attachment Syles (Strange Situation)

Attachment Styles	Behavior During Separation & Reunion
Secure	Distressed when caregiver leaves; easily comforted upon return.
Insecure-Avoidant	Shows little distress; avoids caregiver upon return.
Insecure-Resistant (ambivalent)	Very distressed; seeks contact but resists comfort. Clingy and hard to soothe.
Disorganized	Confused, fearful, or contradictory behavior. Often linked to trauma or neglect.

Epilogue

From Surviving to Teaching

I used to think survival was the goal. That if I could just make it through the next crisis, the next court date, the next eviction, I'd finally arrive. But survival is only the beginning. What comes after—the healing, the reckoning, the rebuilding—that's where the real work begins.

This memoir is not just my story. It's a curriculum. A case study. A mirror for students, practitioners, and anyone trying to understand what trauma looks like from the inside—and what transformation feels like when it's earned.

I've lived every theory I studied. I've walked through Erikson's stages with a fractured identity, climbed Maslow's hierarchy with no food in the fridge, and wrestled with Freud's model of the id, the ego and superego in real time. I didn't learn these concepts in a vacuum—I learned them in jail cells, foster homes, and family courtrooms. And now, I teach them not just with a degree but with lived experience.

To my children: You are the proof that cycles can be broken. You've seen me rise, fall, and rise again. You've watched me turn pain into purpose, and purpose into policy. You are my legacy, and this book is your inheritance.

To my readers: If you've made it to this page, thank you. Thank you for witnessing. Thank you for learning. Thank you for believing that stories like mine belong in classrooms, boardrooms, and policy tables—not just in whispered corners.

I am no longer just surviving. I am teaching. I am leading. I am writing. And I am free.

Glossary of Developmental Theory Terms

Adler's Birth Order Theory. Proposed by Alfred Adler, this theory suggests that a child's position within the family (oldest, middle, youngest) influences personality development, coping strategies, and identity formation. Birth order dynamics can shape feelings of belonging and self-worth.

Ainsworth's Attachment Styles. Building on Bowlby's work, Ainsworth identified three primary patterns of attachment—secure, avoidant, and ambivalent (later expanded to include disorganized). These styles emerge from early caregiver interactions and often predict relationship patterns in adulthood.

Autonomy vs. Shame and Doubt (Erikson's). Toddlers seek independence. Support fosters autonomy; harsh punishment or neglect fosters shame and self-doubt. This stage is often disrupted in system-involved families.

Bowlby's Attachment Theory. Proposes that secure attachment to a primary caregiver is foundational to emotional regulation, social competence, and resilience. Insecure or disrupted attachment can leave children more vulnerable to trauma's effects.

Concrete Operational Stage (Piaget). A stage (ages 7–11) where children begin logical thinking about concrete events. Stability and education are key to developing this stage fully.

Egocentrism (Piaget–Preoperational Stage). A child's inability to see perspectives other than their own. Common in early childhood but prolonged in children who lack emotional modeling or secure attachment.

Environmental Trauma. Chronic exposure to unsafe or unstable environments that shapes emotional, social, and developmental outcomes.

Erikson's Psychosocial Stages. A theory of human development across eight stages, each marked by a core conflict (e.g., Trust vs. Mistrust, Identity vs. Role Confusion). Successful resolution leads to psychological strengths; unresolved stages can echo into adulthood.

Formal Operational Stage (Piaget). Begins around age 12; involves abstract thinking and hypothetical reasoning. Often delayed in children facing chronic instability or trauma.

Freud's Psychosexual Stages. A controversial theory proposing that early childhood experiences shape personality through five stages (Oral, Anal, Phallic, Latency, Genital). While dated, some concepts—like repression and defense mechanisms—still inform trauma theory.

Hypervigilance (Trauma Response). A state of heightened alertness to perceived threats, often resulting from trauma exposure. Hypervigilance can lead to anxiety, exhaustion, and difficulty relaxing, as the body remains primed for danger.*(New — directly supported by van der Kolk, 2003.)*

Identity vs. Role Confusion (Erikson's). Adolescents explore who they are. Supportive environments foster identity; instability, trauma, or systemic involvement can lead to confusion and fragmented self-concept.

Industry vs. Inferiority (Erikson's). School-aged children strive for competence. Success builds confidence; repeated failure or lack of support fosters feelings of inferiority.

Initiative vs. Guilt (Erikson's). Preschool-aged children begin asserting power and control. Encouragement builds initiative; criticism or suppression leads to guilt and hesitation.

Intimacy vs. Isolation (Erikson's). Young adults seek deep relationships. Those with unresolved earlier stages may struggle with vulnerability and connection, leading to isolation.

Kohlberg's Moral Development Theory. Outlines how individuals reason about right and wrong across three levels: Preconventional, Conventional, and Postconventional. Trauma and systemic factors can stall or complicate moral reasoning.

Maslow's Hierarchy of Needs. A motivational theory structured like a pyramid:

- Physiological
- Safety
- Love/Belonging
- Esteem
- Self-Actualization

Unmet lower-level needs (like food or safety) can block emotional and cognitive growth.

Postconventional Level (Kohlberg). A stage of principled reasoning, where abstract ethical principles (justice, human rights) guide decisions—even against rules or authority. Rarely achieved without stability, reflection, and supportive environments.

Preconventional Level (Kohlberg). Morality is based on avoiding punishment or seeking rewards. Common in early childhood but can persist in environments where survival dominates.

Protective Factors (Trauma Theory). Conditions or relationships that buffer individuals from the harmful effects of trauma and stress. Protective factors—such as stable caregivers, safe environments, and community support—promote resilience and recovery.

Repression (Freud). A defense mechanism where painful memories or emotions are pushed out of conscious awareness. Common in trauma survivors and often revisited in healing work.

Self-Actualization (Maslow). The highest level of human development—becoming one's fullest self. In this memoir, it's reflected in legacy-building, storytelling, and advocacy.

Self-Concept. An individual's perception of themselves, influenced by attachment, feedback, and lived experience.

Strange Situation (Ainsworth). A structured observation where infants are briefly separated and reunited with caregivers. Their responses highlight attachment style, from secure comfort-seeking to avoidant or ambivalent distress.

Toxic Stress (Developmental Psychology). A term used to describe chronic activation of the body's stress-response system due to prolonged adversity—such as abuse, neglect, or instability—without adequate support. Over time, toxic stress can alter brain architecture and emotional regulation. *(New — you referenced this in your section on environmental trauma; covered by Maslow [1943], Bowlby [1982], and van der Kolk [2003].)*

Trust vs. Mistrust (Erikson's). The first stage (infancy), where consistent care builds trust. Inconsistent or neglectful caregiving can lead to deep mistrust and difficulty in forming secure relationships later in life.

About the Author

Charlietta Owens is a social worker, storyteller, and cycle-breaker whose life journey spans from system involvement to systemic reform. Born in Gary, Indiana and raised in Minnesota, she survived childhood neglect, poverty, and incarceration—then rose to become a fierce advocate, program manager, and county-level Child Protection Worker for families navigating the very systems she once endured.

She holds an associate's degree in human services, a bachelor's in social work (summa cum laude), and a master's in social work (cum laude), earned as a child welfare scholar, she went on to obtain her licensure as graduate social worker (LGSW), and Certified Trauma Professional (CTP). Her academic journey began way before prison, but survival mode took over the will to focus and obtain college credits. It wasn't until she was behind bars, where only 2 college credits became the first bricks in a new foundation. Today, she blends lived experience with professional expertise to mentor others, shape policy, and teach developmental theory through the lens of endurance and healing.

Charlietta is a wife, mother, sister, daughter, caretaker, and now a curriculum developer who believes that memoir can be pedagogy. Her writing is raw, reflective, and rooted in purpose—designed to help students, practitioners, and community members understand trauma not just as theory but as testimony.

Visit Website: Ypmtmovement.com or Yourpainmytrauma.com

References

Bretherton, I. (1992). The origins of attachment theory: John Bowlby and Mary Ainsworth. Developmental Psychology, 28(5), 759–775. https://doi.org/10.1037/0012-1649.28.5.759

Bowlby, J. (1982). Attachment and loss: Retrospect and prospect. American Journal of Orthopsychiatry, 52(4), 664–678. https://doi.org/10.1111/j.1939-0025.1982.tb01456.x

Erikson, E. H. (1963). Youth: Change and challenge. Child Development, 34(1), 23–31. https://doi.org/10.2307/1126465

Freire, P. (1970). Pedagogy of the oppressed. New York, NY: Herder and Herder.

Freud, S. (1961). The ego and the id (J. Strachey, Ed. & Trans.). New York, NY: W. W. Norton & Company. (Original work published 1923)

Huitt, W., & Hummel, J. (2003). Piaget's theory of cognitive development. Educational Psychology Interactive. Valdosta, GA: Valdosta State University. https://www.edpsycinteractive.org/topics/cognition/piaget.html

Kohlberg, L. (1973). The claim to moral adequacy of a highest stage of moral judgment. Journal of Philosophy, 70(18), 630–646. https://doi.org/10.2307/2025030

Maslow, A. H. (1943). A theory of human motivation. Psychological Review, 50(4), 370–396. https://doi.org/10.1037/h0054346

Piaget, J. (1952). The origins of intelligence in children (M. Cook, Trans.). New York, NY: International Universities Press. (Original work published 1936)

van der Kolk, B. A. (2003). The neurobiology of childhood trauma and abuse. Child and Adolescent Psychiatric Clinics of North America, 12(2), 293–317.

https://therapeuticcare.ie/wp-content/uploads/2019/05/The-neurobiology-of-childhood-trauma-and-abuse.pdf

www.ingramcontent.com/pod-product-compliance
Lightning Source LLC
LaVergne TN
LVHW022035200926
848481LV00003B/703